CAR RECORD BREAKERS

THIS IS A CARLTON BOOK
Text, design and illustrations
Copyright © Carlton Books Limited 2016, 2018

Author: Paul Virr
Executive Editor: Alexandra Koken
Design: Jake da'Costa & WildPixel Ltd.
Cover Design: WildPixel Ltd.
Production: Charlotte Larcombe

First published in 2016 by Carlton Books Limited
An imprint of the Carlton Publishing Group,
20 Mortimer Street, London, WIT 3JW.
This edition published in 2018.

10 9 8 7 6 5 4 3 2 1

A catalogue record for this book is available
from the British Library.

ISBN: 978-1-78312-380-3
Printed in Dubai

CAR
RECORD BREAKERS

FASTEST!

BIGGEST!

MOST EXTRAVAGANT!

CARLTON KiDS

PAUL VIRR

🏆 ABOUT THE AUTHOR

Children's author Paul Virr has written on subjects ranging from dinosaurs to computers and now turns his talents to record-breaking cars. Regrettably his only taste of the Le Mans circuit was in an ancient camper van – no records were broken.

CONTENTS

CAR RECORD BREAKERS

★ ★ ★ ★ ★

RECORD-BREAKING CARS

When you think about record-breaking cars, of course it is the land speed record that first comes to mind. The sheer thrill of speed has captured the imagination of motoring enthusiasts from the earliest days. The pursuit of ever-greater speeds continues today, from land-speed record cars, through to motorsports and the latest supercars.

High-speed cars deliver excitement, hitting the headlines, the record books, or both. However there's a lot more to record-breaking cars than speed alone. Looking at other car records and motoring firsts tells a fascinating history of cars, from the first horseless carriage to the first solar-powered car and beyond.

MAKING MOTORING HISTORY

Cars are so much a part of our everyday lives that it is easy to overlook what a marvel of engineering even the most modest and sensible family car represents. The history of cars is one of continuous innovation and experimentation, with the latest technology, new fuels, engines or materials all being incorporated into pioneering car designs. The result is a long series of motoring firsts, a series of cars that are all record-breakers in one way or another.

499 HLX

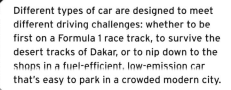

Different types of car are designed to meet different driving challenges: whether to be first on a Formula 1 race track, to survive the desert tracks of Dakar, or to nip down to the shops in a fuel-efficient, low-emission car that's easy to park in a crowded modern city.

⏱ TURNING THE WHEELS

In 2002 archaeologists working in the marshes of Slovenia unearthed the world's oldest wheel. Made of wood and with a wooden axle, it belonged to a prehistoric cart that rolled along muddy tracks more than 5,000 years ago. That cart, like all wheeled vehicles for thousands of years, relied on the muscle power of animals to provide the power to move.

Fast-forward to the nineteenth century and new fuels provided a new way to move along on wheels and axles. Steam power led the way and continued to be a power source for cars in the early days of motoring, competing with newer electric and petrol-powered engines. New fuels led to new engines and car designs, a process that continues today with fuel-cell cars, experimental solar-powered cars, electric cars and hybrids.

Yet however advanced the technology or innovative the design, cars are still doing the same job as that wooden wheeled cart from 5,000 years ago: overcoming friction, drag and gravity to get us where we want to go more quickly. And breaking the odd record along the way.

The Jaguar E-Type is a legendary 1960s sports car. It was one of the first production cars to use a new body construction technique based on that used for building racing cars.

FIRST SUPERSONIC CAR

THRUST SUPERSONIC CAR (SSC)

When Thrust SSC broke the world land speed record on 15 October 1997, it also became the first car to break the sound barrier. Finally the motoring world had its first supersonic car.

The speed of sound in dry air is around 1,200 km/h (760 mph). Thrust SSC beat this with a top speed of 1,228 km/h (763 mph). This meant that when it was running at top speed, Thrust SSC was travelling faster than the noise made by its engines. This super-streamlined car took just half a minute to reach maximum speed, powered by two Rolls-Royce Spey jet engines. These gave Thrust SSC the engine power of about 145 Formula 1 racing cars!

 JET POWER

Turbofan jet engines use a giant fan to draw air into the engine at high pressure, where it is mixed with the fuel and burnt. The exhaust gases, together with some of the air drawn in by the fan, blast out from the rear of the engine, creating forward thrust. A jet engine requires less fuel than a rocket engine, which reduced the weight of fuel Thrust SSC had to carry.

HOW A JET ENGINE WORKS

Huge rotating fan blades draw air into the engine

Hot gases blast out and thrust the aircraft forward.

Spinning blades compress the air and pump it into the combustion chamber.

Fuel burns in the combustion chamber, producing hot gases.

STAYING GROUNDED

To achieve supersonic speed on land, the engineers that built Thrust SSC had to overcome one very difficult challenge to that involved in building supersonic aircraft - keeping the car on the ground! With this in mind, the car was designed with its heavy twin engines mounted at the front, to stop its nose lifting off the ground at high speed.

A jet plane style tailplane keeps Thrust SSC running straight and creates some downforce to keep the car grounded, too.

The aluminium front wheels are fixed either side of the engines at the front. Twin rear wheels are mounted one in front of the other like a bicycle, and are used to steer the car.

THRUST SSC

WHEN	15 October 1997
LENGTH	16.5 m (54 ft)
WIDTH	3.7 m (12 ft)
WEIGHT	10.5 tonnes (11.6 tons)
TOP SPEED	1,228 km/h (763 mph)
ACCELERATION	0-1,000 km/h (0-620 mph) in 16 seconds
FUEL CONSUMPTION:	0.2 km/litre (0.47 mpg)
POWER	82,000 kW (110,000 hp)
ENGINES	Two Rolls Royce Turbofan Jet engines

Thrust SSC broke the sound barrier almost 50 years after the first supersonic flight.

BREAKING THE SOUND BARRIER

As a vehicle approaches the speed of sound, air resistance builds to create a powerful force of drag known as the sound barrier. Breaking through the sound barrier creates a loud shockwave called a sonic boom. Unfortunately, Wing Commander Andy Green, who drove Thrust SSC on its record-breaking 22.5-km (14-mile) run, was unable to hear the thunder-like sonic boom as he was inside the vehicle creating the sound.

FIRST CAR ON THE MOON

LUNAR ROVING VEHICLE (LRV)

U.S. astronauts David Scott and James Irwin took off-road driving to a whole new level on 31 July 1971, taking the Lunar Roving Vehicle for the first off-planet drive - on the surface of the Moon.

The Lunar Roving Vehicle or Moon Buggy was the first of three electric-powered vehicles used by U.S. astronauts to explore the surface of the Moon. These lightweight, high-tech cars were carried by the Apollo 15, 16 and 17 missions to extend the range that the astronauts could travel from their landing sites.

Apollo 15 astronaut Jim Irwin with the Lunar Roving Vehicle on its first trip across the lunar landscape to Elbow crater.

EXTRATERRESTRIAL CAR DESIGN

Among the design challenges the LRV engineers faced were lack of oxygen to run a standard internal combustion engine on the Moon, extreme temperatures, gravity just $\frac{1}{6}$ of the Earth's and the rough terrain of the lunar surface. On top of this, the vehicle also had to fold up into a small size to be transported to the Moon in a spacecraft. Despite all these challenges, it took just 17 months to build the first LRV.

LUNAR ROVING VEHICLE

WHEN	31 July 1971
LENGTH	3.1 m (10 ft 2 in)
WEIGHT	210 kg (463 lb) on Earth 35 kg (77 lb) on the Moon!
PAYLOAD	490 kg (1,080 lb)
WHEELBASE	2.3 m (7 ft 6 in)
TYRES	Zinc-coated steel wire-mesh to grip the dusty surface of the Moon
ENGINES	Two 36-volt batteries powering four motors (one for each wheel)
TOP SPEED	13 km/h (8 mph)
RANGE	65 km (40 miles)

Journeys from the landing site were limited to a distance of about 9.5 km (6 miles) so that the astronauts could walk back in case of vehicle failure.

The four-wheeled LRV was designed to carry two astronauts, their tools, scientific equipment, communications gear and samples of Moon rock. It was also a mobile TV and camera platform.

Three journeys, known as traverses, were made with the LRV on the Apollo 15 mission.

In total the LRV for Apollo 15 covered a distance of 27.8 km (17.3 miles) on the Moon's surface.

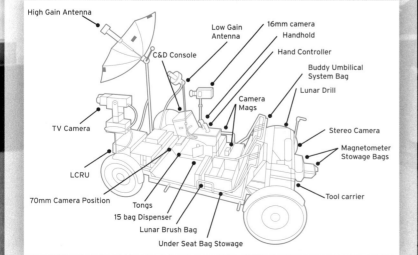

High Gain Antenna
Low Gain Antenna
16mm camera
Handhold
C&D Console
Hand Controller
Buddy Umbilical System Bag
Lunar Drill
Camera Mags
TV Camera
Stereo Camera
LCRU
Magnetometer Stowage Bags
70mm Camera Position
Tongs
15 bag Dispenser
Tool carrier
Lunar Brush Bag
Under Seat Bag Stowage

FIRST MOTOR CAR

BENZ MOTORWAGEN

Horse-drawn carts and carriages ruled the roads until the discovery of petrol in the 1850s.

Although many engineers had seen the potential for self-powered vehicles (or automobiles), they had used steam or electricity as a power source. It was petrol that finally made it possible for the German inventor Karl Benz to build the first practical motor car.

The engine was mounted horizontally at the rear of the Motorwagen and power was transmitted to the rear axle by two chains.

PETROL POWER

Karl Benz developed stationary petrol-powered internal combustion engines in the 1870s. These engines harnessed the explosive force created by petrol when it burns. His next step was to use his petrol engine to power a motorised vehicle. Benz built the first Benz Patent-Motorwagen, the Model 1, in 1885. He received a patent for his invention the following year, making the Motorwagen officially the world's first motor car.

Benz made continuous improvements to his three-wheeled Motorwagen following the success of the Model 1 in 1886.

ON THE ROAD

The three-wheeled Motorwagen made motoring history with its first public test drive in Mannheim, Germany, in July 1886. The Model 1 Motorwagen was not designed for long journeys, so it had neither a fuel tank or brakes, but these were added to later models. In August 1888, Benz's wife Bertha drove a Model 3 Motorwagen 106 km (66 miles) from Mannheim to Pforzheim to visit her mother. This was the first proper long-distance road trip in history. There were no petrol stations, so she had to stop off at pharmacies along the way to buy bottles of petrol.

Instead of a steering wheel, you used a handle to turn the front wheel.

The frame was made of tubular steel, like a bicycle. Benz had previously worked at a bicycle factory.

BENZ PATENT-MOTORWAGEN MODEL 3

WHEN	1886 to 1894
LENGTH	2.7 m (8 ft 10 in)
WHEELBASE	1.6 m (5 ft 3 in)
KERB WEIGHT	360 kg (794 lb)
TOP SPEED:	20 km/h (12.4 mph)
FUEL CONSUMPTION:	0.21 km/litre (0.5 mpg)
POWER	1.1 kW (1.5 hp)
ENGINE	Rear-mounted, single-cylinder, 4-stroke engine
NUMBER PRODUCED:	25

The wheels of the Model 1 had metal rims, wire spokes and solid rubber tyres. The Model 3 had wooden-spoke wheels, with iron rims for tyres.

The first illustration of a Benz motor car journey, published in 1888.

FIRST CAR SALE

Benz sold his first Motorwagen in 1887 to a French bicycle maker called Emile Roger, who later sold Motorwagens from his bicycle shop in Paris. This made the Motorwagen the world's first commercially produced car, or production car, with 25 Motorwagens being produced.

FASTEST ROAD CAR FROM 0 TO 100 KM/H

PORSCHE 918 SPYDER

When it comes to acceleration, the 2015 Porsche 918 Spyder even has the edge over the Bugatti Veyron 16.4 Super Sport, clocking up a time of 2.6 seconds to get from 0 to 100 km/h (62 mph).

This two-seater sports car is the world's quickest-accelerating production car to date.

The car's body is aerodynamically shaped for high speed, with low drag and high downforce.

HYPERHYBRID POWER

The Porsche 918 Spyder is an all-wheel drive hyperhybrid car, powered by a 4.6-litre (280 cu in) V8 internal combustion engine and a pair of electric motors. These provide 115 kW (154 hp) of drive power at the rear axle and 95 kW (127 hp) at the front axle. The ultra-quick response of the electric drive helps to give the 918 Spyder its incredibly fast acceleration from a standing start.

The engine is mounted to the mid-rear, optimizing weight distribution for turning, braking and accelerating.

PORSCHE 918 SPYDER

WHEN	2013-present
LENGTH	4.64 m (15 ft 3 in)
WHEELBASE	2.73 m (8 ft 11 in)
KERB WEIGHT	1,700 kg (3,750 lb)
TOP SPEED:	345 km/h (214 mph) (150 km/h (93 mph) with electric drive only)
ACCELERATION	0-100 km/h (0-62 mph) in 2.6 seconds
FUEL CONSUMPTION	32.26 km/litre (75.88 mpg)
POWER	More than 652 kW (874 hp) maximum system power
ENGINE	One 447 kW (600 hp) V8 combustion engine, plus two electric motors with a combined power of 210 kW (282 hp)
NUMBER PRODUCED:	918

Forged one-piece alloy or magnesium wheels are strong yet lightweight.

SMART ACCELERATION

The 918 Spyder's amazing acceleration is achieved with automated control systems that make the most of its powerful engines and precision engineering. A computerized launch control system ensures the efficient transfer of power to all four wheels. This gives maximum traction between the wheels and the ground and boosts acceleration.

The monocoque outer skin is mostly made from ultra-lightweight carbon-fibre reinforced plastic.

The load-bearing part of the chassis is also made from carbon-fibre reinforced plastic.

SPEEDY SPYDER

In September 2013, a racing version of the Porsche 918 Spyder (41 kg (90 lb) lighter) sped around Germany's Nürburgring in 6 minutes 57 seconds. This made it the first road-legal production car to beat the 7-minute lap record.

BEST-SELLING SPORTS CAR

MAZDA MX-5

Small and lightweight, the Japanese Mazda MX-5 was designed as a lightweight, convertible two-seat sports car that would deliver the same high-speed "wind in your face" thrills as classic roadsters of the past.

Launched in 1989, it has gone on to become the best-selling sports car ever, with more than 940,000 MX-5s produced and sold around the world so far.

Hoods for this convertible were either "hard-top", made from aluminium, or "soft top" made of cloth.

The lightweight body of the first generation MX-5 NA was entirely made of steel.

A BLAST FROM THE PAST

Although open-top roadsters had been around since the earliest days of motoring, it was the appeal of later classic convertibles from the 1960s that originally inspired the Mazda MX-5. Taking inspiration from iconic cars such as the Lotus Elan, research for the MX-5 (short for Mazda Experiment Project 5) started in 1982. But it took until 1989 to make the dream of creating a truly modern roadster a reality.

With two doors, two seats and no wasted space, the MX-5 is every bit the small sports car.

BEST-SELLER LIST

When the Mazda MX-5 was first shown to the public at the Chicago Auto Show in 1989, it was the star of the show, but nobody guessed that it would go on to become the best-selling two-seater convertible sports car in history. With the fourth generation MX-5 ND's release in 2015 that record may be safe for some time to come.

BEST-SELLING CLASSIC ROADSTERS

1. Mazda MX-5 (1989-present): **940,000**

2. Porsche 911 (1963-present): **820,000**

3. Triumph Spitfire (1962-1980): **314,332**

4. BMW Z3 E36/7 (1995-2002): **279,273**

5. Honda S2000 (1999-2009): **112,642**

6. Alfa Romeo Spider (1966-1993): **110,128**

7. Jaguar E-Type (1961-1975): **72,529**

8. Lotus Elan Type 26 (1962-1973): **9,000**

MAZDA MX-5 NA (FIRST GENERATION)

WHEN	1989 to 1997
LENGTH	3.95 m (12 ft 11 in)
WHEELBASE	2.27 m (7 ft 5 in)
KERB WEIGHT	940 kg (2,070 lb)
TOP SPEED	203 km/h (126 mph)
ACCELERATION	0-100 km/h (0-62 mph) in 8.1 seconds
FUEL CONSUMPTION	12.8 km/litre (30.1 mpg)
POWER	86 kW (115 hp)
ENGINE	1.6 litre (98 cu in) 4 cylinder

The MX-5 NA had retractable pop-up head lamps.

FASTEST NON-BOOSTED ROAD CAR

Keeping weight to a minimum gives the F1 a combination of high-speed and excellent road handling.

MCLAREN F1

Launched in 1992, the McLaren F1 remains one of the greatest supercars of all time. The F1 used McLaren's experience in building Formula 1 racing cars to set a new benchmark for the construction and performance of a production sports car. With a top speed of 386 km/h (240 mph), the McLaren F1 is still the fastest production car on the road with a non-turbo or non-supercharged engine.

To shield the carbon-fibre body shell from the heat created by the engines, reflective gold foil was used in the engine bay.

The wheels are made from lightweight magnesium alloy.

NATURALLY ASPIRATED ENGINE

Car engines need air to burn fuel. Top performance cars use superchargers and turbochargers, which squeeze more air into the cylinders to boost engine power. The downside of "boosted" engines is that they are more complex and can be less reliable. For this reason, racing car designer Gordon Murray used a non-turbo BMW engine for his new sports car, the F1. Thanks to its lightweight and super-streamlined design, the F1 didn't need a boosted engine to be very, very fast.

ROAD CAR MEETS RACE CAR

Weight was kept to a minimum on the McLaren F1 by using carbon fibre-reinforced plastic for the car's chassis. The F1 was the first road car with an all-in-one moulded carbon fibre bodyshell called a monocoque. This strong, yet lightweight chassis design provided the framework for the F1's gearbox and engine. Carbon-fibre was lighter and stronger than aluminium, and had previously been used in Formula 1 racing cars.

MCLAREN F1

WHEN	1992-1998
LENGTH	4.29 m (14 ft)
WIDTH	1.82 m (6 ft)
WHEELBASE	2.72 m (8 ft 11 in)
KERB WEIGHT	1,130 kg (2,491 lb)
TOP SPEED	386 km/h (240 mph)
ACCELERATION	0-96 km/h (0-60 mph) in 3.2 seconds
FUEL CONSUMPTION	6.6 km/litre (15.5 mpg)
POWER	468 kW (627 hp)
ENGINE	6.1 litre (372 cu in) BMW V12
NUMBER BUILT	106

K40 MCL

Even the car's included toolkit is made from titanium rather than steel to reduce weight.

Lighter and more powerful GT versions of the McLaren F1 went on to become race champions, including a legendary Le Mans victory in 1995, where McLaren F1 GTRs took first, third, fourth, fifth and thirteenth place!

FIRST CAR FOR THE MASSES

FORD MODEL T

In the early days of motoring, cars were expensive. There were very few cars on the roads as only the wealthy could afford to own one. That changed with the introduction of the Ford Model T in 1908.

Thanks to a new automated way of building cars, Henry T. Ford had finally been able to realize his dream of putting the world on wheels with a truly affordable car.

The rear-wheel drive Model T had three gears: two forward and one reverse.

MASS PRODUCTION

Early cars were slow and expensive to make because they were largely hand-built, one at a time. Each car was built from the chassis up on the same spot by skilled mechanics and craftsmen. American car manufacturer Ransom E. Olds was the first to introduce mass-production with the Curved Dash Oldsmobile. Each car was put together from standard parts, moving along an assembly line where workers fitted the same parts on each car before it passed along to the next stage in the process.

FORD MODEL T	
WHEN	1908 to 1927
LENGTH	3.4 m (11 ft 2 in)
WHEELBASE	2.54 m (8 ft 4 in)
KERB WEIGHT	540 kg (1,190 lb)
TOP SPEED	72 km/h (45 mph)
FUEL CONSUMPTION	5.5 to 9 km/litre (13 to 21 mpg)
POWER	15 kW (20 hp)
ENGINE	2.9 litre (177 cu in), four-cylinder
NUMBER BUILT	15,000,000

ONE CAR FOR ALL

Henry T. Ford had wanted to create a "universal car", low-priced and easy to maintain. Cutting production costs meant that the Model T was the cheapest car around and anyone with a decent salary could buy one. The Model T brought the motor car to the masses and by the 1920s, more than half the cars on the planet were Ford Model T's. In total, more than 15 million Model T's were built and sold around the world.

The bodywork was made of sheet steel.

The flexible chassis and suspension were ideal for travelling on the uneven roads and rough tracks of the time.

The engine could be started by turning a crank handle.

The wheels on the early models had wooden spokes like cartwheels.

FULL SPEED AHEAD

Henry T. Ford took mass production to another level with the Model T at his factory in Highland Park, Michigan, USA. He added automated conveyor belts to move the cars speedily along the assembly line. The assembly line started with a bare chassis and finished with a working car that could be driven away. All these improvements meant that at Highland Park a complete Model T car rolled off the production line every 3 minutes.

LONGEST VINTAGE CAR

BUGATTI ROYALE

Italian automobile designer Ettore Bugatti dreamed up the Bugatti Type 41 Royale as a luxury vehicle to compete against big names such as Rolls Royce. Designed to make a big statement, the Royale's size and elegance were impressive.

At 6.4 m in length, it was the world's longest four-wheeled production car, until the launch of the Mercedes-Maybach S-Class Pullman at the Geneva Motor Show in 2015. Ettore Bugatti would keep the first-ever production model of the Bugatti Royale as his personal car for the rest of his life, but the rest of the world was not so keen. In the end only six of the planned 25 Royales were built.

Each Bugatti Royale has a standing elephant mascot as its radiator cap.

GIANT ENGINE

The Royale's engine block was made of cast iron and has a straight 8 design, which means that all its cylinders were lined up in a row (in comparison, a V8 engine has 4 pairs of cylinders mounted alongside each other in a V shape). Those 8 cylinders had a combined capacity of 12.7 litres (774 cubic inches), and the Royale's engine remains one of the largest production car engines of all time. The engines were so powerful that when the Royale failed to sell in large numbers, the remaining 23 engines were used to power trains for the French national railway.

LONGEST LUXURY FOUR-WHEEL TOP THREE

1. 1927-33 Bugatti Type 41 Royale: **(6.4 m) (21 ft)**

2. 1932-7 Duesenberg SJ: **(6.25 m) (20 ft 6 in)**

3. 1934-5 Cadillac V16: **(6.096 m) (20 ft)**

BUGATTI ROYALE (TYPE 41)

WHEN	1927 to 1933
LENGTH	6.4 m (21 ft)
WHEELBASE	4.3 m (14 ft 1 in)
KERB WEIGHT	3,178 kg (7,006 lb)
TOP SPEED	120 to 125 km/h (75 to 78 mph)
ACCELERATION	0-100 km/h (62 mph) in 18 to 20 secs
FUEL CONSUMPTION	1 km/litre (2.35 mpg)
POWER	224 kW (300 hp)
ENGINE	12.7 litre (774 cu in) straight 8 cylinder engine
NUMBER BUILT	6

Each Royale was a one-off, with custom-made bodywork.

Although the Royale's huge engine was mounted up front, it was rear-wheel drive.

The 61-cm (24-inch) aluminium wheels also made a style statement.

MOST EXPENSIVE CAR IN THE WORLD

FERRARI 250 GTO

Today's high-end production sports cars come with a staggering price tag attached, but it was a blast from the past by Ferrari that once took the record for being the most expensive car ever.

At an auction in October 2013, a 1963 Ferrari 250 GTO sold for more than £31.5 million ($50.5 million). This broke the previous most-expensive car record of over 34 million Euros ($42.5 million), which was paid for another Ferrari GTO in a private sale in 2012.

The interior of the GTO is completely no-frills, without carpets and with bare door panels. The instrument panel has the bare essentials, but there's no speedometer!

The inset headlights are covered with curved plexi-glass to maintain the GTO's streamlined shape.

A COLLECTOR'S CAR

What makes a car collector part with such a huge sum of money for a car built at the start of the 1960s? Firstly, there's the car itself. The lightweight Ferrari 250 GTO has the speed and handling to deal with both the racetrack and the road. It also has one of the sleekest and most eye-catching sports car designs of all time. Added to this is the sheer rarity of these classic sports cars. Just 39 were built in the two years the Ferrari 250 GTO was produced. So whenever one comes up for auction car collectors battle it out and are willing to pay the price for a very drivable piece of motoring history.

Semi-circular panels in the front of the car can be removed to boost cooling.

THE WORLD'S TOP FIVE OTHER MOST EXPENSIVE AUCTION CARS

1. **1954 Mercedes Benz W196**
sold for **£26.1 million** in 2013 ($29.6 million)

2. **1957 Ferrari 250 Testa Rossa**
sold for **£14.4 million** in 2011 ($16.4 million)

3. **1957 Ferrari 250 Testa Rossa**
sold for **£10.9 million** in 2009 ($12.4 million)

4. **1936 Mercedes Benz 540K Roadster**
sold for **£10.4 million** in 2013 ($11.8 million)

5. **1961 Ferrari 250 GT California SWB Spider**
sold for **£9.6 million** in 2008 ($10.9 million)

FERRARI 250 GTO

WHEN	1962-1964
LENGTH	4.3 m (14 ft 1 in)
WIDTH	1.6 m (5 ft 3 in)
WHEELBASE	2.4 m (7 ft 11 in)
KERB WEIGHT	880 kg (1,940 lb)
TOP SPEED	298 km/h (185 mph)
ACCELERATION	0-96 km/h (0-60 mph) in 5.4 seconds
FUEL CONSUMPTION	6.1 km/litre (14.4 mpg)
POWER	220 kW (295 hp)
ENGINE	3 litre (181 cu in) V12
NUMBER BUILT	39

The GTO's sleek bodywork was constructed from aluminium panels, riveted to a tubular steel frame.

A rear spoiler helps to create downforce, keeping the back of the car grounded.

1960s RACING LEGEND

Built to win the new GT World Championship in 1962, the Ferrari 250 GTO was designed to go head-to-head with other classic sports cars such as the E-Type Jaguar and the AC Cobra. Lightweight construction and a powerful V12 engine were combined with a super-streamlined shape, fully-tested in wind tunnels at Pisa University, to make the Ferrari 250 GTO a winner. It went on to win three times in a row at the GT World Championships in 1962, 1963 and 1964, plus it took two wins in its class at Le Mans.

MOST POPULAR CAR MODEL

The five-seater Beetle was designed for families.

VOLKSWAGEN BEETLE

Launched in 1938 and going into full-scale production in 1945, the Volkswagen Beetle, with its distinctive curved shape, has been a familiar sight on roads all around the world ever since.

That's because the Beetle went on to become one of the best-selling car models in motoring history. In 1981 it became the first car to have sold 20 million units. Production only stopped in 2003, by which time more than 21.5 million Beetles had been sold.

The Beetle has the longest production history of a single car model ever.

BFU 607K

Weltmeister

A CAR FOR THE PEOPLE

Austrian car designer Ferdinand Porsche was asked by the German government to create an affordable and reliable mass-produced car. He came up with the Beetle: a two-door, rear-wheel drive car, designed for high-speed driving on the planned network of new roads called the Autobahn. As a car for everyday people, the Beetle was designed to use little fuel and given a curved front and rear shape to reduce air resistance.

TOP FIVE BEST-SELLING CARS

1. Toyota Corolla (1966 to present): 40 million
2. Ford F-Series (1948 to present): 34 million
3. Volkswagen Golf (1974 to present): 25 million
4. Volkswagen Beetle (1945 to 1978): 21 million
5. Vaz – 2101 (1970 to 1988): 19 million

RUNNER UP

Although other cars such as the Toyota Corolla have sold more than the Beetle, these cars have many different models. Other than the name, modern versions look like completely different vehicles from the original, while the original Beetle kept its easily recognizable shape throughout production.

The engine was made from a lightweight metal alloy and mounted at the back of the car where you would normally expect the boot to be. The bonnet at the front lifted to provide storage.

The curved metal bodywork was attached to the chassis with 18 bolts.

VOLKSWAGEN TYPE 1 (VW BEETLE)

WHEN	1938 to 2003
LENGTH	4.1 m (13 ft 5 in)
WIDTH	1.5 m (4 ft 11 in)
WHEELBASE	2.4 m (7 ft 11 in)
KERB WEIGHT	840 kg (1,852 lb)
TOP SPEED	115 km/h (71 mph)
ACCELERATION	0-100 km/h (0-62 mph) in 27.5 seconds
FUEL CONSUMPTION	14.9 km/litre (6.7 l/100 km for standard 25 kW engine)
POWER	25 kW (33.5 hp)
ENGINE	1.2 litre (3 cu in) flat 4 engine
NUMBER BUILT	21.5 million

THE WORLD'S FIRST AMPHIBIOUS CAR

AMPHICAR MODEL 770

Amphibious vehicles can travel both on land and across water. The first amphibious cars were military vehicles, but it wasn't until 1961 that the world got its first mass-produced amphibious car: the Amphicar Model 770.

Built in Germany, the Amphicar was designed for the American market, where the popularity of beach and outdoor leisure pursuits would make its ability to drive on land and water appealing. More than 3,000 Amphicars were shipped to the United States between 1961 and 1967, but the relatively expensive Amphicar never really caught on and production ended in 1968.

Amphicars came in four water-themed colours: Lagoon Blue, Beach White, Fjord Green and Regatta Red.

TRULY CONVERTIBLE

Powered by a British Triumph Herald engine mounted at the rear, the Amphicar has a twin transmission, which can drive either the car's rear wheels, the two propellers at the back, or both at the same time. With its low-set wheels providing a good 253 mm (10 inches) of ground clearance, the car can be driven straight out of the water by starting the wheels turning as it approaches land.

AMPHICAR MODEL 770

WHEN	1961 to 1968
LENGTH	4.3 m (14 ft 3 in))
WIDTH	1.6 m (5 ft 2 in)
WHEELBASE	2.1 m (7 ft)
KERB WEIGHT	1,054 kg (2,324 lb)
TOP SPEED	110 km/h (70 mph) on land; 13 km/h (8 mph) on water
ACCELERATION	1-100 km/h (0-62 mph) in 23 seconds
FUEL CONSUMPTION	14.8 km/litre on land, 6.8 litres per hour on water
POWER	32 kW (43 hp)
ENGINE	1.147 litre (700 cu in) straight 4 Triumph Herald engine
NUMBER BUILT	About 4,000

CHANNEL CROSSING

The Amphicar, with its watertight steel body, was designed to be fully seaworthy. It even has extra navigation lights like a ship or a boat to make it visible to other vessels. On 16 September 1965, two Amphicars left the harbour at Dover and made the sea voyage across the channel from England to France. It was an exciting crossing. Both cars had to drive through high waves, the teams had to refuel by hand in rough seas and then one car broke down and had to be towed by the other! The crossing took 7 hours and 20 minutes.

A two-door convertible, the Amphicar's roof can be folded back, making it even more like a boat.

Twin propellers made from nylon powered the Amphicar through the water like a powerboat.

For driving on water, the side windows could be fully wound down and the doors were made watertight with rubber seals.

The car's front wheels acted as a rudder to steer the Amphicar on water.

FASTEST CAR ON THE ROAD

BUGATTI VEYRON 16.4 SUPER SPORT

Officially the fastest street-legal car on the road, the Bugatti Veyron Super Sport set a new world speed record of 431.072 km/h (268 mph) in 2010, the same year that it was launched.

Aerodynamic, relatively lightweight and with a huge turbocharged engine, the Super Sport was engineered with extreme speed in mind. In fact it goes so fast that the speed is electronically limited to 415 km/h (258 mph) for road use in order to stop its super-wide tyres wearing out! Only 30 of these legendary supercars have been built, with production stopping in 2011. There have been many challengers for the speed record since then, but none have officially beaten the Super Sport.

MAXED-OUT MOTOR

The source of the Bugatti Veyron Super Sport's colossal speed is its huge 8-litre (488 cu in), 16-cylinder engine. With twice the number of pistons as are found in most supercars, it's essentially two V8 engines combined. As if the engine capacity was not enough, the Super Sport has not just one, but four turbochargers to squeeze more air into - and more power out of - those pistons. The result of all this engine power is an incredible rate of acceleration. The four-wheel drive Super Sport can hit a speed of 100 km/h (62 mph) in just 2.5 seconds!

Specially designed tyres help the Super Sport grip the road at speed.

KEEP IT COOL

Naturally all that engine power creates a lot of heat, so the top of the Super Sport's engine is exposed to the air to help cool it. Additional cooling comes from two air ducts under the headlights, two aerodynamically designed air ducts on the roof and three engine radiators (the Super Sport has 10 radiators in total!).

The Super Sport's carbon-fibre monocoque body shell is lightweight and aerodynamic.

BUGATTI VEYRON 16.4 SUPER SPORT

WHEN	2010 to 2011
LENGTH	4.5 m (14 ft 7 in)
WIDTH	1.9 m (6 ft 2 in)
WHEELBASE	2.7 m (8 ft 10 in)
KERB WEIGHT	1,838 kg (4,052 lb)
TOP SPEED	431 km/h (268 mph)
ACCELERATION	0-100 km/h (0-62 mph) in 2.5 seconds
FUEL CONSUMPTION	4.3 km/litre (10.1 mpg)
POWER	882 kW (1,200 hp)
ENGINE	8-litre (488 cu in), quad turbocharged, 16 cylinder engine
NUMBER BUILT	30

The Veyron is named after Pierre Veyron, one of the drivers that won Le Mans in 1939, driving a much earlier Bugatti car.

SLOW IT DOWN

When it comes to braking from extreme speeds the Veyron Super Sport also has it covered, thanks to specialist engineering. As well as its carbon-fibre reinforced ceramic disc brakes, the rear spoiler can also be angled to act as an air brake. These help the Super Sport to slow down from 100 km/h (62 mph) to a standstill in a distance of just 31.4 metres (103 feet).

At 220 km/h (137 mph) the Super Sport automatically lowers its body to just 9 cm (3.5 in) off the ground, which together with the rear spoiler helps to create downforce, keeping the car on the road.

SMALLEST MICRO CAR

PEEL P50

Measuring just 1.4 m (54 in) long and 0.99 m (39 in) wide, the three-wheeled Peel P50 microcar is the world's smallest production car. Designed for city driving, the Peel 50's size makes it easy to park in crowded urban areas.

Designed by Cyril Cannell and built from 1962 to 1965 by Peel Engineering Limited on the Isle of Man, everything about the Peel P50 was cut back to keep size to a minimum. It had just one door (on the left-hand side), one headlight, one windscreen wiper and one seat for the driver.

MINI MOTORING

The Peel P50 has a small 0.49-litre (3.0-cu-in) single-cylinder Zweiral Union engine. These were essentially German-made moped engines and though not capable of high speeds, are ideal for a car designed for small runs in town. There was no speedometer and no electric starter motor: you fire up the Peel P50 by pulling on a cranking handle. The fan-cooled engine has a three-speed gearbox, but no reverse gear! If you want to back into a parking space, you simply get out and use a chrome-plated handle at the rear of the car to lift and move the car into position.

The Peel 50 had no chassis – its body shell was made from welded tubular steel and lightweight fibreglass.

PEEL

MIGHTY MICROCARS

The trend for small and economical single-seater cars that started after the Second World War continued into the 1960s. These small vehicles became known as microcars and included futuristic designs with domed roofs and windshields that were affectionately known as bubble cars.

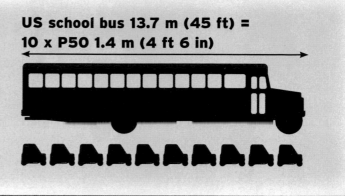

US school bus 13.7 m (45 ft) =
10 x P50 1.4 m (4 ft 6 in)

The original Peel P50s from the 1960s are very rare and fetch high prices at car auctions.

PEEL P50

WHEN	1962 to 1965
LENGTH	1.4 m (4 ft 6 in)
WIDTH	0.99 m (3 ft 3 in)
WHEELBASE	1.3 m (4 ft 2 in)
KERB WEIGHT	59 kg (130 lb)
TOP SPEED	60 km/h (37 mph)
FUEL CONSUMPTION	35.7 km/litre (84 mpg)
POWER	3.4 kW (4.6 hp)
ENGINE	0.49 litre (3.0 cu in), single cylinder engine
NUMBER BUILT	47

The P50 was available in four colours: Daytona White, Dragon Red, Capri Blue and Sunshine Yellow.

In 2011 production of a new range of modern Peel P50s began, including electric-powered models.

The Peel's wheels are less than 13 cm (5 in) in diameter.

LONGEST LIMOUSINE

AMERICAN DREAM STRETCH LIMOUSINE

American Dream was a one-off stretch limousine built by ex-stunt driver and car collector Jay Ohrberg in 1992. At more than 30 metres (100 feet) in length, it holds the world record for the longest car ever built.

American Dream was a stretch limousine conversion and was constructed from two 1977 Cadillac Eldorado convertibles. The front of each Cadillac was fitted to either end of a massively extended chassis, complete with 26 wheels! Costing $10,000 dollars a day to hire out, demand for American Dream unfortunately didn't pick up. The car fell out of use and is now in storage. However, Jay Ohrberg plans to build an even longer limousine in the future.

It was claimed that 50 people could squeeze into the interior of the American Dream.

The swimming pool and helicopter pad were located in this end section.

A DIFFERENT CLASS OF CAR

Limousines have always been luxury cars in a class of their own. Designed to be driven by a chauffeur and with a separate and roomy passenger compartment, the interior of a limousine is usually fitted out with the best that money can buy for travel in comfort and style. From their early days limousines have usually had a long wheelbase, but modern stretch limousines have taken this further with extended chassis models built by a number of luxury car manufacturers or with the conversion of luxury cars by independent coachbuilders.

The middle section could be converted to bend like a long "bendy" bus.

DRIVING THE DREAM

With two engines and two driving compartments, American Dream could be driven from either end, which made reversing such a long vehicle easier. Cornering could be tricky in city streets, so American Dream was designed so that it could be converted to bend in the middle. It could even be split into two sections for transportation by truck over long distances.

AMERICAN DREAM STRETCH LIMOUSINE

WHEN	1992
LENGTH	30.5 m (100 ft)
WIDTH	2 m (6 ft 6 in)
KERB WEIGHT	10,000 kg (22,046 lb or 11 tons)
FUEL CONSUMPTION	0.35 km/litre (0.82 mpg)
POWER	298 kW (400 hp)
ENGINE	Two 7-litre (427 cu in) V8 engines (one each end)
NUMBER BUILT	1

ADDED EXTRAS

Designed for use in films and for display at motor shows, American Dream had extras beyond those you'd normally get in limousines. These include a swimming pool, complete with diving board, a jacuzzi, a king-size bed, a satellite dish and even a landing pad for a helicopter.

Large cars can be gas guzzlers – American Dream burnt nearly three litres of fuel every kilometre!

The extended bonnet was just for show and extra length. It housed a standard Cadillac engine.

MOST EXPENSIVE CAR EDITION

BUGATTI LEGENDS ETTORE BUGATTI

The most expensive commercially available car (as opposed to an auction car, or a bespoke, custom-built car) is currently a limited edition version of the Bugatti Veyron 16.4 Grand Sport Vitesse belonging to the Legends series.

Production of this series began in 2013 with the first of six models designed to celebrate Bugatti's motoring history. Each edition (or model) is named after a Bugatti motoring hero: Jean-Pierre Wimille, Jean Bugatti, Rembrandt Bugatti, Meo Costantini, Black Bess (for French racing driver Roland Garros) and Ettore Bugatti, after the founder of Bugatti cars. Just three cars have been built of each edition. The final edition of the Legends series, the Ettore Bugatti was revealed in August 2014. It holds the world record for being the most expensive car in the world, selling for an incredible £2.08 million.

The Ettore Bugatti's two-colour design was inspired by Bugatti's Type 41 Royale of 1932.

RACY ROADSTER

Vitesse is the French word for speed, which suits the Grand Sport Vitesse down to the ground as it is the fastest roadster in the world. This means the Ettore Bugatti version of the Grand Sport delivers proper sports car thrills when driving with the top down. The Ettore Bugatti is capable of incredible speed, but the engine is electronically limited to 375 km/h (233 mph) for use on normal roads.

BUGATTI LEGENDS ETTORE BUGATTI

WHEN	2014
LENGTH	4.5 m (175 in)
WIDTH	1.99 m (78 in)
WHEELBASE	2.7 m (106 in)
KERB WEIGHT	1,990 kg (4,390 lb)
TOP SPEED	410 km/h (255 mph)
ACCELERATION	0-100 km/h in 2.6 seconds (0-60 mph in 2.4 seconds)
FUEL CONSUMPTION	4.3 km/litre (10 mpg)
POWER	880 kW (1,180 hp)
ENGINE	8 litre (488 cu in) 16 cylinder, quad turbocharged
NUMBER BUILT	3

The Ettore Bugatti has a carbon fibre bodyshell, but the front of the car including the bonnet, wings and doors are made of hand-polished aluminium, protected by a clear lacquer coating.

The specially designed wheels are badged with Ettore Bugatti's EB initials.

The Bugatti horseshoe badge and EB logo on the rear are made of platinum.

LONGEST PRODUCTION CAR

MERCEDES-MAYBACH S-600 PULLMAN

First revealed at the Geneva motor show in 2015, the Mercedes-Maybach S-600 Pullman is a limited edition limousine and the second car in the new ultra-luxury Mercedes-Maybach brand.

Designed to compete with other ultra-luxury cars, such as the Rolls Royce Ghost, the S-600 is not for your average motorist. These supersize luxury cars are built for chauffeurs driving VIPs such as heads of state around – and they have a supersize price tag to match. At 6.5 m (21 ft 3 in) in length, the S-600 just beats Bugatti's classic Royale to take the record for the world's longest production car.

The S-600's powerful V12 engine is soundproofed to provide a quiet, luxurious driving experience.

LARGE-SCALE LUXURY

Everything about the S-600 has been done on a grand scale, from its impressive size through to its stunningly luxurious interior. Based on the Mercedes-Maybach S-Class Sedan, the S-600 has a wheelbase that is more than a metre longer. It also adds 100 mm (4 in) of extra headroom for its passengers.

TRAVELLING IN STYLE

The passenger compartment of the S-600 is very spacious and is separated from the chauffeur by an electrically controlled glass partition. This can be raised and lowered, but it can also be changed from clear to opaque at the touch of a switch for complete privacy. In addition to this, stylish curtains for the rear windows help to keep celebrities safe from newspaper photographers. The interior, including the roof, is completely upholstered in leather. S-600 can seat four, with two fully adjustable leather executive seats facing the direction of travel and two pull-down seats facing backwards.

MERCEDES-MAYBACH S-600 PULLMAN

WHEN	2015
LENGTH	6.5 m (21 ft 4 in)
WIDTH	1.9 m (6 ft 3 in)
WHEELBASE	4.42 m (14 ft 6 in)
KERB WEIGHT	approx. 2,406 kg (5,304 lb) (without armour plating)
TOP SPEED	210 km/h (130 mph)
ACCELERATION	0-100 km/h (0-62 mph) in 5 seconds*
FUEL CONSUMPTION	7.75 km/litre (18.2 mpg)
POWER	390 kW (523 hp)
ENGINE	Benz's 6.0-litre (366-cu-in) twin-turbo V 12
	* = approximate value

As a car for VIPs, the S 600 Pullman is likely to have armour-plating and to be heavier and not quite as fast as a standard S-600.

Large rear doors make getting in and out of the S-600 easy.

CREATURE COMFORTS

For entertainment there's a built-in widescreen TV/computer monitor and a top-of-the range sound system. At the touch of a switch a table pops up between the passenger seats, complete with glasses for refreshments. If that's not enough to keep you occupied on long trips, there are also three dials fitted in the roof liner so that passengers can keep an eye on the outside temperature, the car's speed and what time it is.

WORLD'S FIRST TURBOCHARGED CAR

OLDSMOBILE JETFIRE

In 1962, US car manufacturer General Motors released a new version of their F85 Oldsmobile, the Jetfire. On the surface the car looked much the same as a regular F85, but under the bonnet was a revolutionary new development in the history of the internal combustion engine: a turbocharger.

This allowed more power to be squeezed out of the same size of engine and gave the Jetfire a 15% boost in power over the non-boosted (naturally aspirated) engine. The Jetfire was the world's first turbocharged passenger car, closely followed by the Chevrolet Corvair Monza Spyder just a month later. Unfortunately the Jetfire's turbocharger proved unreliable and many Jetfires were converted back to a regular engine.

The Jetfire was a rear-drive hardtop coupé.

TURBOCHARGED ENGINES

Ever since it was invented, engineers, scientists and car designers have been improving the internal combustion engine, trying to make it more efficient or to squeeze more power out of it. One of the ways that the power of an engine can be boosted is by increasing the amount of air pumped into it. If more air can be squeezed into a cylinder it can burn more fuel and create more power. This is exactly what a turbocharger does, compressing (making smaller) the air and forcing more air into the combustion chamber along with the fuel. Turbochargers were first widely used in aircraft from the 1920s onwards, but the technology was later applied to cars.

The bodyshell was made from steel and had angular, jet-age styling.

OLDSMOBILE JETFIRE

WHEN	1962-1963
LENGTH	4.8 m (15 ft 9 in)
WIDTH	1.8 m (5 ft 7 in)
WHEELBASE	2.8 m (9 ft 2 in)
KERB WEIGHT	1,297 kg (2,859 lb)
TOP SPEED	176 km/h (109 mph)
ACCELERATION	0-96 km/h (0-60 mph) in 8.5 seconds
FUEL CONSUMPTION	5 km/litre (11.8 mpg)
POWER	160 kW (215 hp)
ENGINE	3.5-litre (214-cu-in V8 Turbo2
NUMBER BUILT	9,607

The Jetfire was a sportier, two-door version of the Oldsmobile F85.

TURBO TECHNOLOGY

Engines burn a mix of fuel and air. A turbocharger forces more air into the cylinder, which can then be mixed with more fuel to get more power out of the same size cylinder. The clever bit is that the engine uses the power created by its own exhaust gases to compress the air it draws in. The engine's hot exhaust gases turn a fan called a turbine as they exit the engine. This is connected to and rapidly turns another fan called a compressor, which sucks air into the engine and squeezes it into a smaller volume. This air is cooled and then is drawn into the cylinder where it helps the fuel to burn more quickly, generating more power.

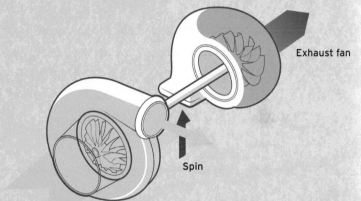

Exhaust fan

Spin

Compressor

The trim on the Jetfire included the two chrome spears on the bonnet.

FIRST JET-POWERED CAR

ROVER JET1

From steam power to nuclear power, car designers have explored many different power sources in the development of the motor car – and have built many different types of engine to make a car's wheels turn round.

Advances in airplane technology during the jet age inspired British car manufacturer Rover to try to replace the internal combustion engine with a gas turbine jet engine. Rover had previously worked on the development of a jet engine for aircraft with its inventor, Frank Whittle, in 1940. Following a series of problems, Rover parted ways with Whittle and turned their attention towards harnessing the same jet technology to power a passenger car. This led to the building of the Rover JET1, a one-off concept car that was the world's first jet-powered car.

The JET1 was a two-door roadster based on the Rover 75.

JET1

TEST DRIVE

Rover started work on developing a small gas turbine jet engine for cars in 1946. Progress was not straightforward and there were various setbacks and even an engine exploding before a successful prototype was built in 1948. Further development of the engine continued and the chassis and bodywork of a Rover 75 was converted to fit the jet engine, creating the two-seater JET1. The car was finally unveiled to the public during a test drive in front of the cameras at the Silverstone racing circuit in the UK on 8 March 1950. In 1952 the car got an engine upgrade and JET1 took the world speed record for a gas turbine car, clocking up a speed of 244 km/h (151 mph) and winning the RAC Dewar trophy.

THE JET THAT DIDN'T TAKE OFF

Although the JET1 worked, it was not easy to drive as it was slow to respond to the controls. On top of that it was very inefficient in its use of fuel. Rover went on to build a gas turbine powered racing car with British Racing Motors, which raced at Le Mans in 1963 as an experimental car. With gas turbine engines being costly to manufacture and expensive to run, the JET1 never became a production car and is now a key museum exhibit at London's Science Museum.

The Rover-BRM gas turbine car that raced at Le Mans.

The gas turbine jet engine was mounted at the rear behind the seats.

Exhaust outlets were on top of the rear section of the car.

ROVER JET1

WHEN	1950
LENGTH	4.5 m (14 ft 9 in)
WIDTH	1.7 m (5 ft 7 in)
WHEELBASE	2.8 m (9 ft 2 in)
TOP SPEED	145 km/h (90 mph)
ACCELERATION	0-97 km/h (0-62 mph) in 14 seconds
FUEL CONSUMPTION	2.5 km/litre (5.9 mpg)
POWER	390 kW (523 hp)
ENGINE	Rear-mounted Rover gas turbine jet engine
NUMBER BUILT	1

WORLD'S SHORTEST PRODUCTION CAR

RENAULT TWIZY

Although officially classed as a heavy quadricyle, and despite its lack of standard doors and windows, the Renault Twizy can be properly considered as an ultra-small electric car. It's not as short as the smallest microcar ever (the Peel P50), but it is a lot shorter and narrower than popular city cars, such as the Smart Fortwo.

In fact, at just 2.3 m (7 ft 7 in) in length, it is currently the world's shortest production car. Designed for crowded cities, the Twizy is a battery-powered two-seater, whose small size and ultra-tight turning circle - 3.4 m (11 ft 2 in) - make parking easy. Its 100 kg (220 lb) 6.1 Kw battery pack can store enough power to give the Twizy a maximum range of 100 km (62 miles) - which is more than enough for short trips running about the city.

The Twizy is a single speed, rear wheel drive car.

The Twizy's battery takes just three and a half hours to fully charge up.

RENAULT TWIZY

WHEN	2012 to present day
LENGTH	2.3 m (7 ft 7 in)
WIDTH	1.2 m (3 ft 11 in)
KERB WEIGHT	474 kg (1,045 lb)
TOP SPEED	80.5 km/h (50 mph)
ACCELERATION	0-48 km/h (0-30 mph) in 8.4 seconds
FUEL CONSUMPTION	Fully electric, zero emission vehicle
POWER	12.7 kW (17 hp)
ENGINE	Electric induction motor
NUMBER BUILT	15,000

SMALL GOES BIG

The Twizy was launched as a concept car at the 2009 Frankfurt Motor Show, but French car manufacturer Renault didn't start producing the Twizy until 2011. Since then it has gone on to become one of the best-selling electric cars in Europe and more than 15,000 have been sold worldwide.

The original Twizy concept car had several features that didn't make it through to the production version, including enclosed wheels.

Tandem seating has the passenger sat directly behind and slightly higher than the driver.

The chassis is made up of a steel frame with built-in crumple zones at the front and back for safety.

Doors don't come as standard, but plastic scissor doors are an optional extra to keep the rain out. They open up and forward.

The Twizy comes with many options for customization, including different colours for the bodywork and the 32.5 cm (1 ft 1 in) alloy or steel wheels.

WORLD'S FIRST FOUR-WHEELED CAR

CANSTATT-DAIMLER MOTORIZED CARRIAGE

In the late 19th century Germany became the world centre of motor car innovation. Although Karl Benz is usually credited with building the first motor car (the three-wheeled Benz Motorwagen), less than 100 km away from his workshop in Mannheim another team of motoring pioneers were developing their own car.

The engine was mounted centrally, just in front of the rear bench seat.

Gottlieb Daimler and his partner Wilhelm Maybach had built the world's first compact high-speed petrol engine in 1885. They called their single cylinder engine the "grandfather clock engine". Having experimented with using it to power a two-wheeled vehicle (the Petroleum Reitwagen) they went on to install a larger version in a modified horse carriage in 1886, creating the Daimler Motorized Carriage – the world's first four-wheeled car. Although the companies founded by Daimler and Benz would later merge, these two car pioneers had developed their inventions independently and never actually met.

Early cars were known as horseless carriages because they were essentially customized horse-drawn carriages, built of iron and wood.

CANSTATT-DAIMLER MOTORIZED CARRIAGE

WHEN	1886
LENGTH	2.5 m (8 ft 2 in)
WIDTH	1.5 m (4 ft 11 in)
WHEELBASE	1.3 m (4 ft 3 in)
KERB WEIGHT	290 kg (639 lb)
TOP SPEED	18 km/h (11 mph)
POWER	0.8 kW (1 hp)
ENGINE	0.1 litre (6 cu in) single-cylinder grandfather clock engine
NUMBER BUILT	1

THE FOUR-STROKE ENGINE

The four-stroke internal combustion engine was originally invented by the German engineer Nikolaus Otto in 1876. Daimler and Maybach had worked with Otto developing stationary engines, but when they fell out with him they left to develop the internal combustion engine for moving vehicles instead. Otto's four-stroke cycle was the foundation of modern car engines.

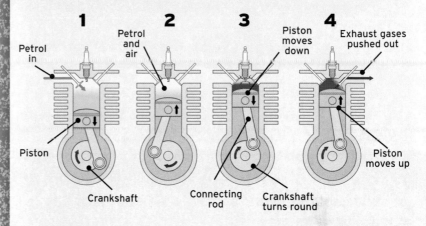

1. Induction: The piston moves down and a valve opens to allow a mixture of air and petrol to be sucked into the cylinder.

2. Compression: The piston moves up, squeezing the mixture, compressing into the small space at the top of the cylinder.

3. Power: A spark ignites the mixture, which expands, pushing the piston down.

4. Exhaust: The piston moves up again, forcing the waste, or exhaust, gases out of the cylinder.

There was no fuel tank, but 2 litres (4 pints) of petrol were used to fill the surface carburettor.

On their way to creating the world's first four-wheeled, four-stroke motor car, Daimler and Maybach built the world's first proper motorcycle, powered by an internal combustion engine: the Petroleum Reitwagen (riding car).

WORLD'S FIRST ROTARY-ENGINED PRODUCTION CAR

NSU SPIDER

German car and motorcycle manufacturer NSU launched a new two-door sports car at the Frankfurt Motor Show in 1964. At first glance, the NSU Spider looked pretty similar to their 1958 two-door sports coupé, the Sport Prinz, however, the Spider was radically different in the engine compartment.

Instead of a conventional internal combustion engine, the Spider had a rotary piston engine, based on the pioneering work of German engineer Felix Wankel.

The engine was rear mounted and accessible under the rear luggage compartment.

THE WANKEL ENGINE

Lighter and smaller than a standard engine of the same power, the Wankel engine had many advantages in theory. Rotary motion made for a smoother-running engine and fewer parts meant that it should have been less expensive to make and less likely to break down. However, in practice the engine suffered from leakages that detracted from its performance and mechanical stresses that made it unreliable. The rotary engine would later be improved and used by Mazda in more successful cars, but the NSU Spider retains its place in motoring history as the world's first rotary-engined production car.

NSU Spiders came in either red or white with a black hard top that could be used for winter.

NSU SPIDER

WHEN	1964-1967
LENGTH	3.6 m (11 ft 10 in)
WIDTH	1.5 m (4 ft 11 in)
WHEELBASE	2.0 m (6 ft 7 in)
KERB WEIGHT	700 kg (1,543 lb)
TOP SPEED	150 km/h (93 mph)
ACCELERATION	0-100 km/h (0-62 mph) in 14.5 seconds
POWER	37-40 kW (50-54 hp)
ENGINE	0.5-litre (30 cu in), single rotor Wankel rotary engine
NUMBER BUILT	2,375

With its fold back roof, the Spider was essentially an open-top version of the NSU Prinz bodyshell.

THE WANKEL ENGINE

Felix Wankel had first started work on his rotary engine in the late 1920s, but it wasn't until 1936 that he finally patented his radical redesign of the internal combustion engine. He came up with an alternative to a standard combustion engine with fewer moving parts. The Wankel engine had an oval-shaped combustion chamber and a curved triangular central rotor that could carry out the same four-stroke process, but with the combustion forces being directly converted into rotary motion.

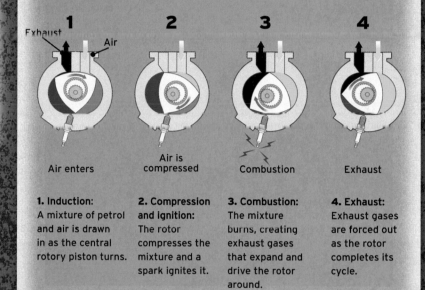

1	2	3	4
Exhaust Air			
Air enters	Air is compressed	Combustion	Exhaust

1. Induction: A mixture of petrol and air is drawn in as the central rotory piston turns.

2. Compression and ignition: The rotor compresses the mixture and a spark ignites it.

3. Combustion: The mixture burns, creating exhaust gases that expand and drive the rotor around.

4. Exhaust: Exhaust gases are forced out as the rotor completes its cycle.

FASTEST-
ACCELERATING ROAD CAR
FROM 0 TO 300 KM/H

KOENIGSEGG ONE:1

Extreme acceleration is a given for supercars, but at a practice run on 8 June 2015, the Koenigsegg One:1 made an incredible unofficial record-breaking run at a test-track in Sweden.

This new version of the Koenigsegg Agera was named "one to one" to match its impressive one-to-one horsepower to weight ratio. It's the world's first car to generate a full megawatt (1,000 kW) of power (1,340 hp) and that's why Swedish car manufacturer Koenigsegg describe it as the world's first megacar. The Koenigsegg One:1 lived up to its promise of stunning power on the test track, beating the world record for a run from 0 to 300 km/h (0 to 186 mph) and back by more than three seconds. It took just 11.92 seconds to accelerate from a standing start to 300 km/h (186 mph) and then 6.03 seconds to brake to a stop, giving a total time of 17.95 seconds for the run.

The Koenigsegg One:1 is a two-door, two seater with a fixed roof.

KOENIGSEGG ONE:1

WHEN	2014 to 2015
LENGTH	4.3 m (14 ft 1 in)
WIDTH	2 m (6 ft 7 in)
WHEELBASE	2.7 m (8 ft 10 in)
KERB WEIGHT	1,360 kg (2,998 lb)
TOP SPEED	439 km/h (273 mph)
ACCELERATION	0-300 km/h (0-186 mph) in 11.9 seconds, 0 to 100km/h (62 mph) in 2.8 seconds
FUEL CONSUMPTION	6.8 km/litre (16 mpg)
POWER	1,000 kW (1,340 hp)
ENGINE	5-litre (305-cu-in) V8 twin-turbocharged engine
NUMBER BUILT	7

TRACK TECHNOLOGY

The Koenigsegg One:1 is a road legal supercar, but it was designed with the track in mind, so every detail has been considered to squeeze the maximum performance out of the car. Even the exhaust outlet is the result of the latest technology and has been 3D printed from titanium in order to save 400 grams (0.88 lb) of weight over one made from aluminium. Electronic control systems and sensors boost performance, for example by actively controlling the height of the car to match the road surface or by adjusting the rear wings to create more downforce at speed.

The One:1 is fitted with custom Michelin Pilot Sport 2 Cup tyres that are specially designed to handle extreme speeds.

All that engine power needs a lot of cooling, so the One:1 has large vents including a roof air scoop.

The car can run on biofuel, racing fuel or regular petrol.

FIRST FOUR-WHEEL DRIVE CAR

The fuel tank was mounted over the rear wheels, behind the two leather upholstered bucket seats for driver and navigator.

SPYKER 60 HP

In 1903 Jacobus Spijker, one of the founders of pioneering Dutch car manufacturer Spyker, commissioned a revolutionary new racing car: the Spyker 60 HP. Designed by a young Belgian engineer called Joseph Valentin Laviolette, the Spyker 60 HP boasted a number of ground-breaking innovations.

For starters, it was the first car in the world to be powered by a six-cylinder engine, designed to give it a power advantage in races. But what made the Spyker truly different was that this engine drove all four wheels of the car at the same time, rather than just the front or rear two wheels. This made the Spyker 60 HP the world's first permanent four-wheel drive, or all-wheel drive, petrol car. What's more, it was also the first car to have brakes for all four wheels.

FOUR-WHEEL WINNER

One of the advantages that a four-wheel drive car has over a two-wheel drive car is increased traction – the force that the tyres can apply to the road. In addition, because all four wheels are driven, even if there's wheel slippage on one wheel, the others can continue to move the car forwards. The Spyker's four-wheel drive system gave it the edge in rainy, uphill conditions and it won its debut competition at the 1906 Birmingham Motor Club Hill Climb in the UK, being one of just a handful of cars to finish the steep uphill course.

SPYKER 60 HP RACING CAR

WHEN	1903
LENGTH	Approx. 3.4 m (11 ft 2 in)
WIDTH	Approx. 1.6 m (5 ft 3 in)
WHEELBASE	Approx. 2.5 m (8 ft 2 in)
TOP SPEED	129 km/h (80 mph)
POWER	44.7 kW (60 hp)
ENGINE	8.8-litre (537-cu-in), 6 cylinder
NUMBER BUILT	1

The Spyker 60 HP also featured another Spyker innovation – a patented dust shield chassis, designed to keep the dust of early unsurfaced roads out of the engine.

The engine was started by inserting and turning a crank handle at the front.

FIRST MASS-PRODUCED FOUR-WHEEL DRIVE ROAD CAR

AUDI QUATTRO

Although civilian versions of four-wheel drive military vehicles, such as Willys Jeep or the Soviet GAZ-61 had been available since the 1940s, it wasn't until the 1980s that a permanent four-wheel drive road car made an impact on the mass market.

That car was the Audi Quattro, which was launched at the Geneva Motor Show in 1980. Designed by Audi engineer Jorg Besinger, the Quattro was inspired by the excellent performance of Volkswagen's four-wheel drive military vehicle in difficult winter driving conditions, the Iltis. Besinger saw that a four-wheel drive could bring Audi success in rallying and yet also be the basis for a commercially successful road car.

Independent front and rear suspension helped the Quattro deal with uneven road surfaces.

The Quattro was a two-door coupé with a steel monocoque bodyshell.

FOUR TO THE FLOOR

The Quattro got its name from the Italian word for "four", referring to its permanent 4-wheel drive. Based on the Audi 80 saloon, it successfully combined a powerful turbocharged five-cylinder engine with the performance advantages of four-wheel drive in a relatively affordable mass-produced vehicle. Audi's development team had come up with a lighter and more efficient four-wheel drive system than anything that had been built previously. Pairing this with a high performance engine proved a winning combination.

AUDI QUATTRO

WHEN	1980 to 1991
LENGTH	4.4 m (14 ft 5 in)
WIDTH	1.7 m (5 ft 7 in)
WHEELBASE	2.5 m (8 ft 2 in)
KERB WEIGHT	1,290 kg (2,844 lb)
TOP SPEED	220 km/h (137 mph)
ACCELERATION	0-100 km/h (0-62 mph) in 7.1 seconds
FUEL CONSUMPTION	9.1 km/litre (21.4 mpg)
POWER	147 kW (197 hp)
ENGINE	2.1-litre (128-cu-in) 5-cylinder turbocharged engine
NUMBER BUILT	11,452

The Audi Quattro A1 (all-wheel drive 1), like all the original models is known as an UrQuattro.

 **RALLY CHAMPION**

In 1981 a change in the rules made it possible to enter four-wheel drive cars in the World Rally Championships. The Quattro's all-wheel drive gave it excellent roadholding and manoeuvrability and Audi won the 1981 WRC in Sweden as well as RAC rallies in Italy and Britain. With more successes the following year, the Audi Quattro was one of the most successful rally cars ever and changed the sport forever.

The engine was front-mounted and most of the car's weight was over the front wheels.

CHAMPION OFF-ROAD
RALLY RAID RACER

MINI ALL4 RALLY RACING CAR

Rally raids are long distance endurance races that push drivers and their cars to their limits. The Dakar Rally is one of the most challenging rally races. Competitors have to cross thousands of kilometres of extreme off-road terrain, including sand dunes, rocky desert trails and mud.

That's why the two-week long Dakar race has become the testing ground for some of the toughest off-road cars ever built. Recently one small and powerful car has dominated the race: the Mini All4 Racing Car. This high-performance all-terrain car is in fact the most extreme mini ever built. It's a four-wheel drive off-road champion that has won the Dakar rally four times in a row from 2012 to 2015. The Mini All4 truly ruled the race in 2015, winning eleven of the thirteen stages and also taking third, fourth, fifth and ninth places in the top ten cars to finish!

BUILT FOR EXTREMES

At first glance the All4 looks like a Mini Countryman, but that's where the resemblance ends. In fact it's a bit bigger than a standard Countryman and only a few details such as the windscreen, door handles and lights come straight from the production car. The rest of the car, from the custom-built tube-steel chassis through to the turbocharged 3-litre (183-cu-in) diesel BMW engine and the carbon-fibre bodywork is put together by rally race team X-Raid in Frankfurt, Germany.

MINI ALL4 RALLY RACING CAR

WHEN	2011
LENGTH	4.3 m (14 ft 1 in)
WIDTH	2.0 m (6 ft 7 in)
WHEELBASE	2.9 m (9 ft 6 in)
KERB WEIGHT	1,905 kg (4,200 lb)
TOP SPEED	180 km/h (112 mph)
ACCELERATION	0-97 km/h (0-60 mph) in 5.5 seconds
FUEL CONSUMPTION	2.24 km/litre (5.27 mpg)
POWER	239 kW (320 hp)
ENGINE	3.0-litre (183-cu-in) BMW six-cylinder turbocharged diesel

The All4 carries three spare wheels on board and has an onboard hydraulic jack system for rapid wheel changes.

The chassis is made from tubular steel and the bodyshell from tough carbon-fibre panels.

The suspension allows each wheel a top-to-bottom movement of 20 cm (8 in), enough to deal with the most uneven off-road surfaces.

The All4 can carry up to 400 litres (105 gallons) of fuel in its tank, which is handy for when there's no petrol station in races through remote regions.

The brakes are water-cooled to cope with extreme use.

WORLD'S UNOFFICIAL SPEEDIEST SUPERCAR

HENNESSEY VENOM GT

At the high end of supercar engineering, manufacturers compete for the top position in various performance records, such as top speed and fastest acceleration times. Some records are officially recognized by strict standards and others are unofficial records, but worthy of note nevertheless.

Especially when it comes to the blistering speed of a car like the Hennessey Venom GT. This two-seat supercar, based on a modified Lotus Exige chassis, showed what it can do with its seven-litre twin-turbocharged V8 engine on February 14, 2014 at the Kennedy Space Center's space shuttle runway. With its incredible power-to-weight ratio, the Venom recorded a top speed of 435.31 km/h (270.5 mph), shattering the current production-car speed record. But as the run was only in one direction and only 16 Venom GTs had been built, the car didn't qualify as a production car for the official record.

The Venom GT previously held a world record for acceleration, clocking up 0 to 300 km/h (0 to 186 mph) in 13.63 seconds.

The suspension system can be automatically adjusted to raise the Venom more than 5 cm (2 in) to provide enough clearance to get over bumps.

TOP TORQUE

The Hennessey Venom GT is also a record-beater when it comes to engine torque. This is a measure of the turning power of an engine and is one of the key factors in determining how fast a car can accelerate. Torque is a measure of the rotating force that the engine applies on the crankshaft. The Venom has a maximum torque of 1,745 N-m (Newton-metres) (1,287 lb-ft). That's more than the Koenigsegg One:1 (1,371 N-m) (1,011 lb-ft) and the Bugatti Veyron 16.4 Super Sport (1,500 N-m) (1,106 lb-ft). Of course the weight of the car, how it is distributed, the tyres and the size of the wheels all play their part too in determining a car's acceleration.

The Venom's lightweight monocoque bodyshell is made from a mix of aluminium and carbon fibre.

The rear-wheel drive Venom has a mid-mounted engine, making sure a good deal of the car's weight is over the rear axles for maximum traction.

The Kennedy Space Center's straight runway is more than 5 km (3 miles) long, and gave the Venom plenty of space to speed up and brake safely.

HENNESSEY VENOM GT

WHEN	2012 to present
LENGTH	4.7 m (15 ft 5 in)
WIDTH	2.0 m (6 ft 7 in)
WHEELBASE	2.8 m (9 ft 2 in)
KERB WEIGHT	1,244 kg (2,743 lb)
TOP SPEED	435.31 km/h (270.5 mph)
ACCELERATION	0-300 km/h (0-186 mph) in 13.63 seconds
POWER	1,082 kW (1,451 hp)
ENGINE	7.0-litre (427-cu-in) twin-turbocharged V8 engine
NUMBER BUILT	16 (29 planned)

FIRST HYBRID CAR

LOHNER-PORSCHE SEMPER VIVUS

Hybrid cars seem like a very modern idea. Running on a mix of electric and petrol power, hybrids can cut fuel consumption and exhaust gas emissions.

A battery-powered electric motor usually powers the vehicle at lower speeds, for example when driving in town, while the petrol engine is used for higher speeds. This technology sounds ultra hi-tech and hybrids are definitely a growing area in modern car development, but the idea for a hybrid electric vehicle actually goes back to end of the nineteenth century. In fact Professor Ferdinand Porsche (who later created the Volkswagen Beetle) is credited with the invention of the world's first practical hybrid car: the Lohner-Porsche Semper-Vivus.

The name Semper Vivus means "always alive" in Latin.

THE LOHNER-PORSCHE MIXTE

In 1901, Porsche improved on the Semper Vivus design to create a proper hybrid production car, the Lohner-Porsche Mixte. With a large 5.5-litre (336-cu-in) four-cylinder engine as a generator and an even smaller battery (and less weight) it was more reliable, but couldn't compete with the ever-improving petrol cars of the time. In the end only eleven were sold and it would take almost a century for car manufacturers to return to the hybrid concept and make it work.

This reconstruction of the prototype Lohner-Porsche Semper Vivus has two front-wheel hub motors. It was unveiled at the New York Auto Show in 2011, 111 years after the original was built!

LOHNER-PORSCHE SEMPER VIVUS

WHEN	1900
LENGTH	3.4 m (11 ft 2 in)
WIDTII	1.9 m (6 ft 3 in)
WHEELBASE	2.3 m (7 ft 7 in)
KERB WEIGHT	1,542 kg (3,400 lb)
TOP SPEED	35 km/h (22 mph)
RANGE	200 km (124 miles)
POWER	1.85 kW (2.5 hp) per cylinder, 2 kW (2.7 hp) per wheel
ENGINES	Two single cylinder De-Dion-Bouton petrol engines, plus four electric wheel-hub motors
NUMBER BUILT	1

ELECTRIC PIONEER

In 1900, at the Paris World Exhibition, Ferdinand Porsche launched the Lohner-Porsche Elektromobil. Battery-powered electric motors directly powered the hubs of its front wheels. He then went on to design an electric racing car with four wheel-hub electric motors. Because battery power limited the range of electric cars, Porsche next added in two petrol engines to create a serial hybrid system for the Semper Vivus. Its two engines drove two generators that powered the wheel-hub electric motors as well as recharging the batteries.

With its exposed engines and lack of bodywork, the Semper Vivus was a concept car more than a production car model.

The introduction of two small petrol engines meant that Porsche could use a smaller battery than in his Elektromobil – and also cut down the car's weight.

FASTEST ELECTRIC PRODUCTION CAR

TESLA ROADSTER

There was a time when battery-powered electric cars (BEVs) were thought of as worthy, environmentally friendly, and possibly a bit dull. But that all changed with a new generation of high-performance all-electric cars, such as the Tesla Roadster, which went into production in 2008.

This two-door roadster has the racy bodyshell of a Lotus Elise and has an electric motor that can do 0 to 97 km/h (0 to 60 mph) in 3.9 seconds. It's fast and is electronically limited to keep it road safe with a top speed of 201 km/h (125 mph). This makes the Tesla Roadster the world's fastest all-electric road car.

The monocoque chassis, which is part of the bodyshell, is made from aluminium and carbon-fibre body panels.

⚡ GREEN DREAM

In 2009, a Tesla Roadster set a world record for the distance travelled by an all-electric car on a single charge. It covered 511 km (317.5 miles) during the Global Green Challenge in Australia without a drop of petrol being burned. Electric cars are environmentally friendly in that they don't produce exhaust gases and don't consume petrol. However they do need to be charged with electricity. A full recharge takes three and a half hours and the electricity used may have been produced by power stations burning fossil fuels that do create emissions.

The Tesla Roadster was the first car to use a new type of battery with lithium-ion cells. Its battery pack weighs in at nearly half a tonne (0.55 tons)!

⚡ ELECTRIC SUPERCARS

Modern all-electric cars can offer all the excitement of petrol-powered supercars, but are cheaper to run and have zero exhaust emissions. Plus a high-performance electric engine is almost silent compared to the roar of a supercar's petrol engine, yet every bit as capable of delivering extreme speed. Another advantage an electric motor has over a standard petrol engine is almost instant acceleration. The rear-mounted electric motor drives the rear-wheels with fewer moving parts than a standard car, making cars such as the Tesla Roadster relatively low maintenance.

There's no reverse gear, the motor just turns in the opposite direction.

Production stopped in 2012, but in 2015 Tesla announced they would be releasing a new version of the Roadster in 2019.

TESLA ROADSTER

WHEN	2008 to 2012
LENGTH	3.9 m (12 ft 10 in)
WIDTH	1.9 m (6 ft 2 in)
WHEELBASE	2.4 m (7 ft 11 in)
KERB WEIGHT	1,335 kg (2,943 lb)
TOP SPEED	201 km/h (125 mph)
ACCELERATION	0-97 km/h (0-60 mph) in 3.9 seconds
RANGE	393 km (244 miles)
POWER	147 kW (197 hp)
ENGINE	375 volt AC Induction Motor
NUMBER BUILT	2,600

LONGEST GRAND PRIX WINNING STREAK

MCLAREN-HONDA MP4/4

One of the most exciting Grand Prix seasons in F1 history was in 1988, when a new car designed by McLaren totally dominated the competition.

That car was the McLaren-Honda MP4/4, which race legends Alain Prost and his team-mate Ayrton Senna drove to victory in fifteen of the sixteen Grand Prix races. That's a record Formula One Grand Prix winning streak that still stands today.

FORMULA ONE CARS

Formula One (or F1) is the highest level of motor racing, where specialized single-seater cars compete on circuits with dramatic left and right turns. F1 cars are the fastest racers in the world, hitting top speeds of up to 360 km/h (223 mph), but they also need to corner at high speed to stay in front on winding racetracks. The name "Formula One" refers to the strict rules (formula) that control how car designers (known as constructors) can build their cars. Within those rules, constructors have pushed car technology to its limits with amazing aerodynamic designs and finely tuned, high-performance engines.

The MP4/4 had a pioneering new design for the driver's bucket seat, which was slanted so that the driver laid back into it. A break from the usual upright driving position, it suited the low-to-the-ground design of the MP4/4 and would later become a standard feature of all F1 cars.

1988 FORMULA ONE MCLAREN-HONDA MP4/4

WHEN	1988
LENGTH	4.4 m (14 ft 5 in)
WIDTH	2.1 m (6 ft 11 in)
WHEELBASE	2.9 m (9 ft 6 in)
KERB WEIGHT	540 kg (1,190 lb)
TOP SPEED	333 km/h (207 mph)
POWER	485 kW (650 hp)
ENGINE	1.5-litre (92-cu-in) Honda twin-turbo V6 engine
NUMBER BUILT	6

FIRST MASS-PRODUCED HYBRID CAR

TOYOTA PRIUS

In 1992, Japanese car manufacturer Toyota announced that it would start development of an environmentally friendly car, with both increased fuel efficiency and low exhaust emissions. Three years later, they unveiled a concept hybrid car at the Tokyo Motor Show. It was called the Prius.

Like the very first hybrid cars built more than a century earlier, it combined a petrol engine and an electric motor. The Prius combined petrol and electric power in a way that was much more energy efficient in a car that was easy to drive. The Prius was launched in 1997 and was the world's first mass-produced hybrid electric vehicle (HEV). Including later versions of the Prius HEV concept, more than three million of this successful family economy car had been sold around the world by 2013.

TOYOTA PRIUS XW10

WHEN	1997 to 2003
LENGTH	4.3 m (14 ft 1 in)
WIDTH	1.7 m (5 ft 7 in)
WHEELBASE	2.6 m (8 ft 6 in)
KERB WEIGHT	1,254 kg (2,765 lb)
TOP SPEED	159 km/h (99 mph)
ACCELERATION	0-100 km/h (0-62 mph) in 13.4 seconds
POWER	33 kW (44 hp) electric motor and 52kW (70 hp) petrol power
ENGINE	1.5-litre (92-cu-in) 4- cylinder petrol engine, plus 273.6 volt electric motor
NUMBER BUILT	123,000

The small petrol engine and electric motor are mounted at the front of the car and drive the front wheels.

THE NEW BREED OF HYBRID

Like all hybrid electric cars, the Prius tries to find an efficient balance between using two types of power. It uses the Toyota Hybrid System (THS), which connects the internal combustion engine, with an electric motor and a generator via a clever power-split device. This is an automatic gearbox that switches between the power sources so that the Prius runs on whatever is most efficient at the time. The Prius starts off using the instant acceleration of the electric motor, but at 64 km/h (40 mph) the petrol engine switches in, driving the front wheels and turning the generator. Then the car can cruise along with a combination of electric and petrol power, drawing on the batteries and the electric motor for any bursts of acceleration.

The Toyota hybrid system is compact and fits in a standard size engine compartment.

The Prius also featured regenerative braking, which harvested the energy created by slowing the car down to generate electricity to recharge the battery.

The Prius is a full hybrid that can be powered by either petrol or electric power, or even both at the same time.

The four-door Prius sedan was the first mass-produced practical hybrid family car.

A powerful battery was located behind the back seats.

LAND SPEED RECORD: STEAM-POWERED CAR

INSPIRATION

Many early cars were powered by steam. In fact, a century ago the world land speed record was held by a steam-powered car. In 1906, American racing car driver Fred Marriott reached a top speed of 204 km/h (127 mph) in a modified Stanley Steamer at Ormond Beach, Florida, USA.

This would be the longest standing land speed record until 2009, more than 100 years later, when a British steam-powered car called Inspiration reached an average speed of 225 km/h (140 mph) at the Edwards Air Force base in the Mojave Desert, USA. Nicknamed the "fastest kettle in the world", the Inspiration achieved the record on 25 August, 2009.

The record breaking speed of 225 km/h (140 mph) was the average of two separate runs, but Inspiration has an even greater theoretical top speed of 274 km/h (170 mph).

THE RISE AND FALL OF STEAM CARS

In the pioneering days of motoring, more Stanley Steamers were sold than cars with internal combustion engines. Known fondly as the "flying teapot" the Stanley Steamer's engine was more reliable than an internal combustion engine, with just fifteen moving parts. Plus there was no need to risk injury using a crank handle to start the car as you did with petrol cars before they had electric starter motors. However, you did have to fire up the boiler half an hour before setting off! Just a few years later, in 1909 the land speed record was taken by Victor Hémery in a Blitzen Benz, powered by a four-cylinder internal combustion engine. It was symbolic of the fall of steam-powered cars and the rise of the ever-improving internal combustion engine. Car designers and steam enthusiasts have yet to find a way to harness the high torque of the steam engine in an efficient way, but it is possible that the dream of a modern steam car could be realized one day.

High-pressure super-heated steam at a temperature of 400°C (752°F) runs through more than 3 km (nearly 2 miles) of copper tubing, driving a twin turbine that powers the rear wheels.

Inspiration has a steel space frame chassis with lightweight carbon-fibre and aluminium body panels.

The water tank is located under the driver's seat and contains enough water for each run. If it ran dry the boilers would melt.

Four disc brakes and a parachute slow Inspiration down.

The steam turbine engine is powered by superheated steam created by 12 liquid petroleum gas fired boilers. Each boiler is about the size of a suitcase and they are mounted in the centre of the car behind the driver's seat.

BRITISH STEAM CAR INSPIRATION

WHEN	2009
LENGTH	7.6 m (24 ft 11 in)
WIDTH	1.7 m (5 ft 7 in)
TRANSMISSION	Rear wheel drive
KERB WEIGHT	3,000 kg (3,614 lb)
TOP SPEED	225 km/h (140 mph)
FUEL CONSUMPTION	73 litres (19 gallons) of liquid petroleum gas (LPG) per 3-minute run
WATER CONSUMPTION	40 litres (10.5 gallons) of distilled water
POWER	268 kW (359 hp)
ENGINE	Two-stage steam turbine powered by 12 LPG fired boilers
NUMBER BUILT	1

FIRST PRODUCTION FUEL-CELL CAR

HONDA FCX CLARITY

In the search for a greener alternative to fossil fuels such as petrol, some car manufacturers have been developing fuel-cell cars. Fuel cells use hydrogen to create on-demand electricity, which then powers the car's electric motor.

Honda had been working on a zero-emission fuel-cell electric vehicle (FCEV) since 1999, but in 2008 their first production model, a four-door family sedan called the Honda FCX Clarity was released. With three times the fuel efficiency of a same-sized standard petrol engine the FCX Clarity went on to win the World Green Car award in 2009. Production of the Clarity stopped in 2014 as Honda prepares to release its next generation fuel-cell car.

The FCX part of the Honda FCX Clarity's name stands for Fuel Cell Experimental.

NOT FOR SALE

You couldn't actually buy the Honda FCX Clarity. It was only released to selected candidates in Japan and the United States (where hydrogen is more easily available) as part of a three-year rental scheme. With each fuel-cell engine costing about ten times as much as that of a standard hybrid or electric car engine to make, this rental scheme provided a way for Honda to test the Clarity out in the real world.

Like standard electric cars, the Clarity uses regenerative braking to generate extra electricity, regaining some of the energy lost as the car slows down.

THE GREEN OPTION?

When hydrogen reacts with oxygen it can release more than double the amount of energy than the same weight of petrol. However, unlike petrol, hydrogen doesn't create potentially harmful exhaust gases, such as carbon dioxide. Instead, the only waste product is ordinary water. The only problem is that hydrogen gas does not occur naturally and sometimes the process used to make it can create pollution. For example, hydrogen can be made from water, but the process uses electricity that may have come from power stations that burn fossil fuels in the first place.

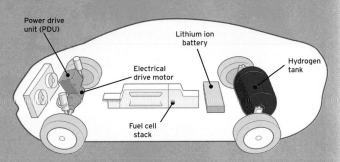

Power drive unit (PDU)

Lithium ion battery

Electrical drive motor

Hydrogen tank

Fuel cell stack

Hydrogen is pumped into the stack of fuel cells where it reacts with oxygen from the air to create electricity and water.

It takes just five minutes to refuel the FCX Clarity with compressed hydrogen. But there are a limited number of hydrogen refuelling stations so use of the car has been limited to specific areas.

HONDA FCX CLARITY

WHEN	2008 to 2014
LENGTH	4.8 m (15 ft 9 in)
WIDTH	1.9 m (6 ft 2 in)
WHEELBASE	2.8 m (9 ft 2 in)
KERB WEIGHT	1,600 kg (3,527 lb)
TOP SPEED	161 km/h (101 mph)
ACCELERATION	0-97 km/h (0-60 mph) in 9.2 seconds
FUEL CONSUMPTION	115.9 km/kilogram (158 miles/lb) of hydrogen
POWER	100 kW (134 hp)
ENGINE	Fuel-cell powered Honda E-Drive electric motor
NUMBER BUILT	200

Compressed liquefied hydrogen gas is highly explosive, so the fuel tank is protected and insulated by an ultra-tough carbon fibre shell. The Honda FCX Clarity can travel more than 350 km (217 miles) on a full hydrogen tank.

With zero exhaust emissions, the Clarity doesn't need an exhaust pipe!

THE FIRST LAND-SPEED RECORD CAR

JEANTAUD DUC ELECTRIC CAR

On December 18, 1898, the world's first land-speed record was set by Count Gaston de Chasseloup-Laubat in an electric car built by the French inventor Charles Jeantaud. The record-breaking 57-second run was made on a cold and rainy day on a kilometre-long (0.62-mile-long) stretch of road outside Paris.

The Count's battery-powered car reached what now seems a modest speed of 63.15 km/h (39 mph), but this was faster than anybody had ever travelled before and was the world's first official land speed record.

JEANTAUD DUC PROFILÉE

WHEN	1899
LENGTH	Approx. 3.1 m (10 ft 2 in)
WIDTH	Approx. 1.2 m (4 ft)
WHEELBASE	Approx. 1.7 m (5 ft 7 in)
KERB WEIGHT	Approx. 1,450 kg (3,197 lb)
TOP SPEED	63.15 km/h (39 mph)
POWER	27 kW (36 hp)
ENGINE	Single electric motor, chain-driven rear wheel-drive
NUMBER BUILT	1

Powered by heavy alkaline batteries the Jeantaud held just enough charge for the record-breaking sprint.

The Jeantaud's single electric motor was connected to the rear wheels with an external chain.

RECORD-BREAKING RIVALS

The Jeantaud's record-breaking run earned Count Gaston de Chasseloup-Laubat the nickname of the Electric Count. It also started a fierce rivalry with Belgian driver Camille Jenatzy, dubbed the Red Devil because of his ginger beard. Just weeks later on January 17, 1899, the two competed in a motoring duel for the title of fastest driver in the world. Jenatzy made the first run in his electric CGA Dogcart and snatched the record away with a speed of 66.66 km/h (41.5 mph). But his victory was short-lived. Minutes later the Count took the record back with a speed of 70.31 km/h (43.5 mph). Over four months the record swapped hands between the rivals. Each driver held the land speed record (no matter how briefly) an amazing three times.

Early cars were usually steered by a horizontal lever like the tiller of a boat, but the Jeantaud electric cars had a handle on a horizontal wheel instead, which gives the Jeantaud Duc a good claim to being the first car with a steering wheel.

The Profilée made the Count the first driver to take the land speed record three times.

JAMAIS CONTENTE

As well as rivalry on the road, a technical battle was fought behind the scenes with improvements being made to the rival electric cars. Jenatzy's last car was a rocket-shaped vehicle powered by two electric motors. Named the Jamais Contente (French for "never satisfied"), its 105.88 km/h (65.79 mph) run claimed the speed record and also made it the first car to reach over 100 km/h (62 mph).

The Jamais Contente doubled the battery power of Jenatzy's previous car with two lead acid batteries.

The bodywork was made of a lightweight metal alloy called partimium.

JAMAIS CONTENTE

WHEN	1899
LENGTH	3.8 m (12 ft 6 in)
WIDTH	1.6 m (5 ft 3 in)
WHEELBASE	Approx. 1.7 m (5 ft 7 in)
KERB WEIGHT	1,450 kg (3,197 lb)
TOP SPEED	105.88 km/h (65.79 mph)
POWER	51 kW (68 hp)
ENGINE	Two direct drive 25 kW (34 hp) electric motors
NUMBER BUILT	1

FIRST DIESEL ROAD CAR

MERCEDES-BENZ 260 D

Early petrol engines were very inefficient, with up to ninety per cent of the energy in the petrol burned being wasted as heat rather than actually moving the car. German inventor Rudolf Diesel came up with an alternative in the 1890s – the diesel engine.

It used diesel fuel rather than petrol, which produces more energy than petrol when it is burned. Like a petrol engine it used a four-stroke cycle, but it had a different way of mixing fuel and air. Although more efficient, diesel engines were heavy and more complicated and expensive to build. They were initially used mainly in ships, trains and trucks, but in 1936 the first diesel production car was launched at the Berlin Motor Show in Germany: the Mercedes-Benz 260 D. This large 4-door passenger car could seat six and was closely followed by a diesel version of the Hanomag Record in the same year.

The 260 D could travel up to 500 km (310 miles) on a single tank of diesel, which was relatively cheap at the time.

IVB · 54851

MERCEDES-BENZ 260 D

WHEN	1936 to 1940
LENGTH	4.4 m (14 ft 5 in)
WIDTH	1.6 m (5 ft 3 in)
WHEELBASE	3 m (9 ft 10 in)
KERB WEIGHT	1,530 kg (3,373 lb)
TOP SPEED	90 km/h (56 mph)
FUEL CONSUMPTION	10.5 km/litre (24.7 mpg)
POWER	33 kW (44 hp)
ENGINE	2.6-litre (159-cu-in), four-cylinder inline diesel engine
NUMBER BUILT	2,000

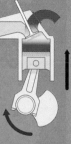 # THE DIESEL ENGINE

Although similar to the four-stroke petrol engine, a diesel engine has a different way of burning fuel to release its energy. It doesn't need spark plugs to ignite its fuel-air mixture. Instead it sucks air into the cylinder and heavily compresses it before it is mixed with the fuel. This makes the air so hot that when diesel fuel is sprayed into the cylinder it explodes without needing a spark. Diesel engines produce less exhaust gases, but create other chemicals that can cause air pollution if they are not removed.

Intake stroke	Compression stroke	Power stroke	Exhaust stroke

1. Intake: The air intake valve opens and the piston moves down, sucking in air.

2. Compression: The piston moves up, compressing the air, which heats up. The piston squeezes the air more than in a petrol engine.

3. Combustion: Diesel fuel is injected into the cylinder as a fine spray. It mixes with the hot air and explodes, forcing the piston down.

4. Exhaust: The piston returns to the top, pushing out exhaust gases as it does so.

The size and weight of a diesel engine made it difficult for early diesel cars to compete with smaller, faster and more smoothly running petrol engines of the time. Until the Mercedes-Benz 260 D, most diesel road vehicles were larger commercial vehicles.

The Mercedes-Benz 260 D's name was based on the 2.6-litre (159-cu-in) capacity of its engine.

The fuel efficiency of the 260 D and its large size made it popular as a taxi in Germany. There was even a special taxi version with seven seats.

MOST EXTREME SIX-WHEEL OFF-ROADER

BRABUS B63S

When four-wheel drive just isn't giving enough off-road power, why not go two wheels better with a six-wheel drive car? That's just what the Brabus B63S does, combining six driven wheels for maximum off-road traction, with a powerful 5.5-litre (336-cu-in)Mercedes-Benz V8 engine to provide extreme off-road power.

Launched at the Frankfurt Motor Show in 2013, this road-legal Sports Utility Vehicle (SUV) mixes the high-tech fixtures and fittings of a luxury car (including TV screens set in the back of the headrests), with tough all-terrain engineering. Based on a Mercedes G63 6x6 G-Wagen, the Brabus B63S upgrades the engine power with larger twin-turbo compressors. The added power means it can make it from 0 to 100 km/h (0 to 62 mph) in just 7.4 seconds, not bad for a car that weighs 3.6 tonnes (4 tons) and can deal with sand dunes as well as city roads.

The cabin interior is fitted out in leather with four individual sport seats.

The body shell is a mix of carbon-fibre and chrome, wi wide carbon fibre wheel arch over the B63S's huge wheel

BRABUS B63S-700

WHEN	2013
LENGTH	5.9 m (19 ft 4 in)
WIDTH	2.1 m (6 ft 11 in)
WHEELBASE	4.2 m (13 ft 9 in)
KERB WEIGHT	3,600 kg (7,937 lb)
TOP SPEED	161 km/h (100 mph)
ACCELERATION	0-100 km/h (0-62 mph) in 7.4 seconds
POWER	515 kW (690 hp)
ENGINE	5.5-litre (336-cu-in) twin-turbo V8 engine
NUMBER BUILT	10

MORE SIX-WHEEL WONDERS

Panther 6 1977
A six-wheeled convertible with a twin turbo 8.2-litre (500-cu-in) V8 engine – only two were ever made!

Tyrell P34 (Project 34) Formula 1 Car 1976
A radical design with two front axles with four small wheels at the front and two standard size wheels at the back. Sadly the P34 was only victorious in one Grand Prix race, coming first and second in the 1976 Swedish Grand Prix.

Covini C6W 2004
A 4.2-litre (256-cu-in) 8-cylinder engine helps this two-door Italian sports car to reach 299 km/h (186 mph) on its six wheels.

No expense has been spared in making this luxury SUV. The air intakes and turbo pipes have gold leaf trimming to help cool air entering the engine.

BRABUS 700

The car has a ground clearance of 460 mm (18 in) for off-road adventures and can ford through streams up to a metre in depth.

FIRST FOLDING CITY CAR

The Hiriko Fold is a one-door, two-seater, all-electric car. The door at the front lifts up for the driver and passenger to climb in.

HIRIKO FOLD

The problem of finding space to park a car in crowded cities is not a new one. Back in 1929, German engineer Engelbert Zaschka came up with a radical solution by inventing a three-wheeled car that could be dismantled and folded up in just 20 minutes.

The folding car idea resurfaced in 2009, when Renault displayed a small two-seater concept car called the Zoom, which had a folding rear wheel mechanism to shorten its wheelbase. A production version of the folding car concept came a step nearer with the Hiriko Fold. In 2012, twenty test models of this folding electric microcar were put into production in Spain before being released for testing in Europe.

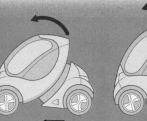

Normal driving mode   Folded up for parking

 FOLDING FOR THE FUTURE

Designed by the Massachusetts Institute of Technology (MIT) in the United States, the Hiriko Fold was designed as part of an environmentally friendly city car project to ease the transport problems of modern cities. The idea is that small, folding electric cars, such as the Hiriko Fold are economical for short-distance urban driving and could reduce traffic, pollution and congestion. The rear axle of the Hiriko Fold is hinged to give it an adjustable wheelbase, with the car body fully extended for driving and then folded up for parking.

HIRIKO FOLD	
WHEN	2012 to present
LENGTH	Switchable between 2.5 m (8 ft 2 in) and 1.5 m (4 ft 11 in)
WIDTH	1.7 m (5 ft 7 in)
WHEELBASE	Variable wheelbase
KERB WEIGHT	700 kg (1,543 lb) with batteries
TOP SPEED	Limited to 50 km/h (31 mph)
ACCELERATION	0-70 km/h (0-44 mph) in 8 seconds
RANGE	120 km (75 miles) on a full battery charge
POWER	15 kW (20 hp)
ENGINE	Four wheel-mounted electric motors
NUMBER BUILT	20

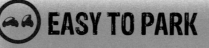 EASY TO PARK

The Hiriko's four "robo wheels" are individually driven by an electric motor and all four can be steered at the same time. They can be be turned much further than standard car wheels so that the driver can manouevre the Hiriko sideways into tight parking spaces. It's also possible to fully rotate the car on the spot.

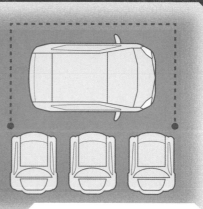

When folded up, three Hiriko Fold cars can park sideways in the space taken up by an average family car.

Powered by batteries, it is a zero-emission car that can travel 120 km (75 miles) between charges.

Instead of a steering wheel, the Hiriko Fold has an airplane-style control column that can be pushed forward to speed up and pulled back to slow down. It can also be moved so you can steer and drive from either the right or left seat.

Engelbert Zaschka's 1929 folding city car had a rear-mounted single cylinder engine and could be folded up into three pieces for space-saving storage.

FIRST PETROL FUEL INJECTION ROAD CAR

MERCEDES-BENZ 300 SL

Car engines burn a mixture of fuel and air to create energy. From the car's earliest days, a mechanism called a carburettor was used to make sure the right mix of fuel and air was created for the engine to run on.

In fact, the carburettor was the usual fuel delivery system for cars until the 1980s, when it was overtaken by a different approach: fuel injection. This involved spraying fuel at high pressure directly into the engine's cylinders. Diesel engines have always used fuel injection, but it wasn't until 1954 that the world's first mass-produced fuel-injection petrol car took to the roads. The car in question was the Mercedes-Benz 300 SL.

This two seater, rear-wheel-drive coupé has become one of the most collectible sports cars.

The standard Mercedes-Benz 300 SL was built with a steel body shell and frame, but 29 cars were made with an aluminium body shell that was 80 kg (176 lb) lighter.

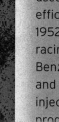 # FASTEST PRODUCTION CAR

The Mercedes 300 SL would go on to become a legendary sports car, combining beautiful styling with raw power. It used a fuel injection system that not only made it more fuel efficient, but gave it a power boost of almost 25% over the 1952 Mercedes-Benz W194 that it was based on (this was a racing version with a carburettor engine). The Mercedes-Benz 300 SL was the fastest production road car of its day and remains one of the most admired sports cars ever. Fuel injection would go on to become standard on petrol-powered production cars from the 1980s onwards.

The 300 SL was a huge success in the United States, where almost four-fifths of the limited production run of these stylish sports cars were exported.

MERCEDES-BENZ 300 SL

WHEN	1954 to 1963
LENGTH	4.5 m (14 ft 9 in)
WIDTH	1.8 m (5 ft 11 in)
WHEELBASE	2.4 m (7 ft 11 in)
KERB WEIGHT	1,093 kg (2,410 lb)
TOP SPEED	260 km/h (162 mph)
ACCELERATION	0-97 km/h (0-60 mph) in 8.8 seconds
FUEL CONSUMPTION	5.9 km/litre (13.9 mpg)
POWER	160 kW (215 hp)
ENGINE	3-litre (183-cu-in), straight six cylinder fuel-injected engine
NUMBER BUILT	1,400

The SL part of the car's name stood for Sports Leicht, which means Sports Light in German.

The twin doors opened upwards, to form a wing shape that gave the car its name – the 300 SL Gull Wing.

WORLD'S FASTEST-ACCELERATING CAR

TOP-FUEL DRAGSTER

When it comes to acceleration, even the most powerful high-performance supercar cannot compete with a top-fuel dragster. These specialized racing cars are engineered with the one aim of achieving the quickest time over a short distance.

A top-fuel dragster burns fuel at the same rate as a huge passenger jet.

With its incredible acceleration, a top-fuel dragster can reach a speed of more than 200 km/h (124 mph) in less than a second. The rear-mounted supercharged engine runs on a highly explosive mix of nitromethane and methanol (basically rocket fuel) and is awesomely powerful, generating more than six times the output of a supercar in an intense burst of energy. The fastest speed recorded by a top-fuel dragster was 540.97 km/h (336 mph), achieved by drag racing legend Tony Schumacher in 2005. A drag race is over in seconds, so although a top-fuel dragster's engine is designed for maximum acceleration, it doesn't need to maintain this for long. Which is a good job, as a dragster's engine would most likely blow up if it had to keep running for more than ten seconds!

HOT WHEELS

To turn all that engine power into forward movement rather than wheel spin, a top-fuel dragster has wide rubber tyres to help it to grip the track. Before the race begins the wheels are spun to warm up the tyres and to lay down a strip of sticky tyre rubber on the drag strip. This is called a burnout and the sticky layer helps to improve the car's traction even more.

A top-fuel dragster's body is long to balance the weight at the rear and to help it drive in as straight a line as possible. The body shell is usually made from lightweight magnesium alloy and carbon fibre.

LENGTH	10.2 m (33 ft 6 in)
WIDTH	1.3 m (4 ft 3 in)
WHEELBASE	7.6 m (24 ft 11 in)
RACE WEIGHT	Approx. 1,052 kg (2,319 lb) including driver
TOP SPEED	529 km/h (329 mph)
ACCELERATION	0-483 km/h (0-300 mph) in 3.05 seconds
FUEL CONSUMPTION	51 litres (13.5 gallons) of fuel per second
POWER	5,966 kW (8,000 hp)
ENGINE	Supercharged 8.2-litre (500-cu-in) V8 engine

As well as powerful rear-wheel disc brakes, top-fuel dragsters use a parachute to slow them down at the end of a race.

Each race is so hard on the engine that some of its components disintegrate. A team of eight mechanics have to completely rebuild the engine between runs and are so skilled that they can do this in about 40 minutes.

A small wing at the front of the dragster creates downforce to keep the front wheels firmly on the track.

SAFEST CAR

VOLVO V40

The first car accident probably dates back to the earliest days of motoring. In 1771, a steam-powered car invented by French engineer Nicolas-Joseph Cugnot ran out of road and crashed into a wall. Thankfully it wasn't capable of doing more than 4 km/h (2.5 mph), so nobody was injured.

However, as cars got faster, the risks increased and car manufacturers started to engineer their cars for safety as well as performance. Passenger protection features such as seatbelts didn't come as standard with cars until the late 1950s. Modern cars are packed with safety features and are fully tested in accident conditions, including head-on crash tests. When it comes to the safest small car on the road, one vehicle has stood out as a solid performer since its launch at the Geneva Motor Show in 2012: the Volvo V40.

VOLVO V40 T5

WHEN	2012 to present
LENGTH	4.4 m (14 ft 5 in)
WIDTH	1.8 m (5 ft 11 in)
WHEELBASE	2.7 m (8 ft 10 in)
KERB WEIGHT	1,582 kg (3,488 lb)
TOP SPEED	250 km/h (155 mph)
ACCELERATION	0-100 km/h (0-62 mph) in 6.3 seconds
FUEL CONSUMPTION	16.9 km/litre (39.8 mpg)
POWER	180 kW (241 hp)
ENGINE	2-litre, inline 4-cylinder turbo petrol engine

The Volvo V40 has many different models, including diesel and cross-country 4x4 versions. The speedy "hot hatchback" version is a compact front wheel drive car with a turbocharged engine.

⊕ CRASH TESTS

Crash tests video what happens when a car hits a concrete barrier head on, or is hit from the side at various speeds. The car is filled with dummy passengers called crash-test dummies. These are packed with scientific sensors to record the effects of the crash. Parts of the crash-test dummies, such as the head and knees, are given a coat of paint before the test to show if any part of the body would come into contact with the car and could cause injury. Other tests show what would happen if a pedestrian was hit by the car to help work out how to minimize the effects of these accidents, too.

The V40 has several airbags to cushion passengers in a collision. The V40 was also the first car to have an airbag that shoots out from under the bonnet to protect pedestrians.

⊕ SAFETY FEATURES

Seat belts and air bags help to slow down the jarring forces of a crash and stop passengers from being hurled forwards through the windscreen. A specially designed crumple zone at the front of the car folds up in a crash, absorbing some of the impact and slowing the car down. Passenger safety cages provide a rigid steel framework that resists crushing if the car rolls over. As well as anti-lock brakes, modern developments in car safety involve smart systems that sense when a crash is about to happen and kick in earlier. There are also computerized systems that help to prevent an accident occurring in the first place, for example by warning of vehicles that are dangerously close or out of sight in the driver's blind spot.

A computerized City Safe system operates at speeds up to 50 km/h (32 mph), with sensors that automatically apply the brakes if there is any danger of a collision.

FASTEST DIESEL ROAD CAR

TRIDENT ICENI MAGNA

With its super-sleek streamlined shape and a seriously powerful 6.6 litre (403-cu-in) turbo-diesel V8 engine, the British-built Trident Iceni is the world's fastest diesel production car and the most fuel-efficient diesel sports car.

Trident's plan to build a two-seater diesel supercar was first announced in 2006, but it took until 2014 and eight prototypes before the car was ready for production. Thanks to a new engine technology that Trident calls "torque multiplication" the Iceni is able to maximize the power it gets from its fuel, better than any other diesel car on the road. It can hit a top speed of 306 km/h (190 mph), yet at everyday speeds the Iceni is incredibly fuel-efficient. Trident claims it can cover more than 3,200 km (1,988 miles) on a single tank of fuel.

The chassis is made from stainless steel to provide a strong framework for the carbon-fibre composite bodyshell, including a curved steel "spine" that runs over the top of the passenger compartment.

TRIDENT ICENI MAGNA

WHEN	2014
LENGTH	*4.3 m (14 ft 1 in)
WIDTH	*1.9 m (6 ft 2 in)
WHEELBASE	*2.6 m (8 ft 6 in)
KERB WEIGHT	*975 kg (2,150 lb)
TOP SPEED	307 km/h (191 mph)
ACCELERATION	0-97 km/h (0-60 mph) in 3.7 seconds
FUEL CONSUMPTION	46 km/litre (108 mpg)
POWER	295 kW (396 hp)
ENGINE	6.6-litre (403-cu-in) turbo-diesel
	*= approximate value

TORQUE MULTIPLICATION

Diesel cars and petrol cars both burn a mixture of air and fuel, but they do it in different ways. In a petrol engine the fuel is mixed with air and then compressed (squeezed into a small space) before it is ignited by a spark to release the energy. In a diesel engine the air is compressed first, which heats it up before a fuel injection system adds the fuel. The Trident Iceni uses a new type of fuel injector to boost the performance of the engine. Basically it allows the fuel and air mixture for each of the eight cylinders to be adjusted as the engine is running to maximize the power output and fuel efficiency.

The Iceni's diesel engine can run on a wide range of fuels including standard diesel, bio-diesel, linseed oil and palm oil.

TOP FIVE FASTEST DIESEL ROAD CARS

1. Trident Iceni Magna - [2016]
306 km/h (190 mph)

2. BMW Alpina D3 Bi-Turbo - [2016]
302 km/h (187 mph)

3. Audi R8 6.0 Quattro V12 TDI - [2009]
299 km/h (185 mph)

4. Porsche Panamera Diesel 3.0 V6 Turbo - [2013]
259 km/h (161 mph)

5. Jaguar XF 3.0D S - [2011]
249 km/h (154 mph)

The Iceni will be available in three models – the Iceni Magna fastback shown here, the Iceni Venturer estate (with extra luggage room) and an open-top convertible sports car with removable roof panels.

The Iceni has front and rear wing cooling vents as well as twin side exhausts.

PRODUCTION CAR WITH THE LARGEST ENGINE

DODGE VIPER SRT

The Dodge Viper was first unveiled as a concept car at the 1989 North American International Auto Show. This powerful two-seater sports car then went on sale in 1992 and has had a long production history that lasts until the present day.

There have been many variations on the original first generation Viper, but one thing that all these different models have in common is a mighty Chrysler V10 engine. With a massive engine capacity of 8.4 litres (513 cu in), the Dodge Viper SRT has the largest engine of any production car.

Dodge claim that the Viper's huge V10 engine creates the most torque of any non-boosted production car engine in the world.

The Viper has white LED headlamps, as well as LED indicators and brake lights.

SUPERSIZE ENGINE

The size of an engine is a major factor in how much power it can create. Engine size is measured by the total volume of all its cylinders in litres or cubic inches – which is basically the amount of space in the engine that can be filled with air and fuel to power the car. The Dodge Viper SRT's all-aluminium V10 engine has a massive 8.4-litre (513-cu-in) capacity, and is capable of generating 477kW (640 hp) of power.

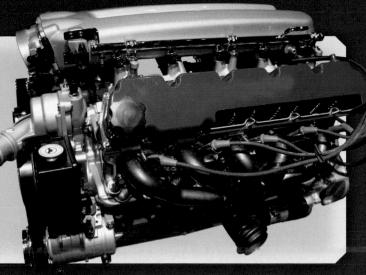

The 2015 Viper has an aerodynamic carbon-fibre body shell with aluminium door panels. The hood that covers the mid-front mounted engine is made as one giant piece of carbon-fibre.

DODGE VIPER SRT (2015)

WHEN	2013 to present
LENGTH	4.5 m (14 ft 9 in)
WIDTH	1.9 m (6 ft 2 in)
WHEELBASE	2.5 m (8 ft 2 in)
KERB WEIGHT	1,521 kg (3,353 lb)
TOP SPEED	330 km/h (205 mph)
ACCELERATION	0-97 km/h (0-62 mph) in 3.2 seconds
FUEL CONSUMPTION	7 km/litre (16.5 mpg)
POWER	477 kW (640 hp)
ENGINE	8.4 litre (513-cu-in) Chrysler V10 engine
NUMBER BUILT	30,000 across 2 generations of models

The first generation of the Dodge Viper's V10 engine was an 8-litre (488 cu in) version that was the powerhouse behind the original Dodge Viper in 1992. The 2015 model with its 8.4-litre (513-cu-in) capacity is the fifth generation of the V10 and produces almost 180 kW (241 hp) more power than the original.

FASTEST SOLAR-POWERED CAR

SUNSWIFT IV

In 1987, the first World Solar Challenge was held in Australia. This was the start of a new type of motor racing, where the competing cars didn't use a single drop of petrol.

That's because they were all solar-powered cars, harnessing the energy of the sun to power them 3,000 km (1,864 miles) from Darwin to Adelaide. The first World Solar Challenge race was won by a General Motors car called Sunraycer, which completed the course in 44 hours and 54 minutes, at an average speed of 66 km/h (41 mph). In the 2009 World Solar Challenge, the Sunswift team from the University of New South Wales in Australia entered their Sunswift IV car (known as Ivy) into the Challenge Class of the race. It finished in 4th place overall, but in 2011, Sunswift IV went on to take the top spot in a different way – by becoming the world's fastest solar-powered car.

SUNSWIFT IV (IVY)	
WHEN	2009 to 2011
LENGTH	4.6 m (15 ft 1 in)
WIDTH	1.8 m (5 ft 11 in)
KERB WEIGHT	165 kg (364 lb) (140 kg (309 lb) without battery pack)
TOP SPEED	88.5 km/h (55 mph) with just solar panels), 95 km/h (59 mph) with solar panels and batteries
POWER	Up to 1.2 kW (1.6 hp)
ENGINE	Single, rear-wheel-drive electric motor
NUMBER BUILT	1

Thanks to its lightweight carbon-fibre chassis the Sunswift IV is less than one tenth of the weight of the average family car.

The battery pack on the three-wheeled Sunswift IV was removed so that it made its record-breaking speed solely on solar power.

WORLD SOLAR CHALLENGE

Designed to promote the development of environmentally friendly, solar car technology, the World Solar Race was held every three years from 1987 until 2001, since when it has been held every two years. Teams from all around the world compete in two main vehicle categories: Challenger Class is for ultra-lightweight and super-streamlined one-seater solar racing cars. Cruiser Class is for more practical cars that might lead to an everyday solar production car being built the future.

SOLAR RECORD BREAKER

On January 7th, 2011, Sunswift IV broke the solar-powered world speed record at an Australian Navy airstrip in Nowra, New South Wales. Over two runs in opposite directions (to cancel out any assistance given by the wind) the car averaged a top speed of 88.5 km/h (55 mph). This was more than 10 km/h (6 mph) faster than the previous record of 78 km/h (48.5 mph), which had been held by the GM Sunraycer for over 20 years.

Petrol-powered cars are very energy-inefficient, with only about 15% of the energy from their fuel being directly used to move the vehicle. Lightweight solar racers like Sunswift IV can turn more than 90% of their solar energy into motion.

ABSOLUTE LAND SPEED RECORD: WHEEL-DRIVEN CAR

BLUEBIRD-PROTEUS CN7

The fastest car on the planet is known as the "absolute" land speed record holder. Until 1963 all the land speed record cars were wheel-driven: the power from their engines turned the wheels to propel the cars along the ground.

Cars that use the thrust from a jet engine or a rocket to drive them along are not wheel-driven – their wheels turn and keep the car connected to the ground, but the wheels don't supply any power to actually move the vehicle. The last wheel-driven car to be the absolute land speed record holder was the British-built Bluebird-Proteus CN7.

Designed for the speed record attempt on a straight track, Bluebird had a limited amount of steer.

DONALD CAMPBELL: RECORD BREAKER

On July 17, 1964, Donald Campbell drove Bluebird on two record-breaking runs across the salt flats of Lake Eyre in Australia. Despite the rain having made for less than ideal driving conditions, Bluebird achieved an average speed of 648.73 km/h (over 403 mph) to take the official land speed record. Later that year, on the very last day of 1964, Campbell set the water speed record with his Bluebird K7 boat to become the only person to hold both the land and water speed records in the same year.

Campbell had previously attempted the speed record in an earlier version of Bluebird at the Bonneville Salt Flats, USA in 1960. The attempt ended in a high-speed crash that seriously injured Campbell and wrecked the car, except for its engine. Campbell slowly recovered and Bluebird was rebuilt around the same engine.

BLUEBIRD- PROTEUS CN7

WHEN	1960-1964
LENGTH	9.1 m (29 ft 10 in)
WIDTH	1.7 m (5 ft 7 in)
WHEELBASE	4.1 m (13 ft 5 in)
KERB WEIGHT	4,064 kg (8,960 lb)
TOP SPEED	710 km/h (441 mph) (peak speed)
POWER	3,320 kW (4,452 hp)
ENGINE	Bristol-Siddeley Proteus 705 free-turbine turboshaft gas turbine
NUMBER BUILT	1

WHEEL-DRIVEN GAS POWER

Bluebird was built around a huge Bristol-Siddeley Proteus turboprop gas turbine originally designed for airliners. The turbine was mounted in the middle of the car within a steel framework that also housed the driver's compartment and the huge 1.3 m (4 ft 3 in) diameter wheels. The car was four-wheel drive with its gas turbine driving both the front and rear axles by means of two drive shafts, one either end of the turbine.

The streamlined bodyshell of Bluebird was built around a steel frame with a honeycombed aluminium chassis that was then covered with alloy panels.

The airtake at the front of the car funnelled air into the engine via ducts that branched either side of the driver's compartment.

The driver's compartment was right at the front of the car and was covered by a forward-hinged canopy made from a strong see-through plastic called perspex.

LAND SPEED RECORD: ELECTRIC CAR

VENTURI BUCKEYE BULLET 2.5

The very first land speed record was set in 1898 by an electric car. Just a year later, another electric-powered car became the first car to travel at a speed over 100 km/h (over 62 mph). More than 100 years later, an all-electric car such as the Tesla Roadster can hit a top speed of 201 km/h (125 mph).

Pretty impressive, but not enough to make it the fastest electric car on the planet. In 2010 that honour went to the Venturi Buckeye Bullet 2.5 (VBB 2.5), a battery-powered electric racer built by engineering students from Ohio State University, USA. On 24 August 2010, the Venturi Buckeye Bullet 2.5 achieved a top speed of 495 km/h (over 307 mph) on the Bonneville Salt Flats, USA. This smashed the 394 km/h (245 mph) world land speed record for battery electric vehicles set in 1999 by White Lightning and made the Venturi Buckeye Bullet officially the fastest electric car in the world.

To slow down the car at the end of its run a parachute is deployed from the back of the car.

The Venturi Buckeye Bullet 3 was built to out-perform its predecessor.

VENTURI BUCKEYE BULLET 2.5

WHEN	2010
LENGTH	11 m (36 ft 1 in)
WIDTH	1 m (3 ft 3 in)
KERB WEIGHT	2,359 kg (5,200 lb)
TOP SPEED	495 km/h (308 mph)
POWER	600 kW (805 hp)
ENGINE	Front-mounted battery-powered electric motor
NUMBER BUILT	1

THE LATEST MODEL

The Venturi Buckeye Bullet 2.5 used the same chassis as its predecessor, which ran on a hydrogen fuel cell. The 2.5 however, was entirely battery powered, using powerful lithium ion battery packs weighing 363 kg (800 lb) in total. Together these are capable of delivering more than 600 kW (805 hp) of power. The 2.5 version of the Venturi Buckeye Bullet took the world record, but was really a test platform for new battery and power technology as the team progressed towards building the Venturi Buckeye Bullet 3. VBB 3 has been developed to try and break its predecessor's record. In 2016 it achieved 549.43 km/h (341.26 mph) on the Bonneville Salt Flats, USA.

The Venturi Buckeye Bullet also goes by the nickname of the "Jamais Contente", which is the same as that of Camille Jenatzy's electric car, the first electric ca to exceed 100 km/h (62 mph).

The VBB 2.5 's electric motors drive the front wheels only. The VBB 3 is a four-wheel drive car.

The chassis is made from a chromoly (containing chromium and molybdenum) steel framework, covered with carbon-fibre body panels. A 1.5 m-high (5-ft-high) rear tailfin helps to keep the VBB running straight.

TURI

LAND SPEED RECORD: FIRST THRUST-POWERED CAR

SPIRIT OF AMERICA

The 1960s saw a game-changing leap in the technology used for land speed record cars. A switch from engines that powered the wheels to thrust-powered cars, where jet or rocket engines provided the forward drive, saw a massive advance in the speed records that could be achieved.

Breaking with the power limitations of wheel-driven cars, these jet and rocket-powered cars redefined what was possible for the land speed record. Record speeds would increase by more than 50% with the latest jet cars such as Thrust SSC. However, the very first thrust-powered car to become the fastest car in the world was Spirit of America, a jet-powered three-wheeler driven by Craig Breedlove. On September 5th, 1963, Spirit of America reached a speed of 657 km/h (408 mph) on the Bonneville Salt Flats, setting the bar high for a new era of speed record-breaking cars.

SPIRIT OF AMERICA

WHEN	1963
LENGTH	11.7 m (38 ft 5 in)
WIDTH	3.5 m (11 ft 6 in) at rear wheels
WHEELBASE	5.8 m (19 ft)
TOP SPEED	657 km/h (408 mph)
FUEL CONSUMPTION	0.09 km/litre (0.2 mpg)
THRUST	23,130 N (5,200 lbf)
ENGINE	General Electric J-47 turbojet engine
NUMBER BUILT	1

GOOD YEAR

SPIRI

The steering wheel had a limited amount of steer and turned both the front wheel and a fin beneath the nose of the car. This fin deflected air to help increase the steer.

THRUST-POWERED RECORD BREAKERS

DATE	DRIVER	CAR	ENGINE	SPEED
5 Aug. 1963	Craig Breedlove	Spirit of America	Turbojet	657 km/h (408 mph)
2 Oct. 1964	Tom Green	Wingfoot Express	Turbojet	665 km/h (413 mph)
5 Oct. 1964	Art Arfons	Green Monster	Turbojet	699 km/h (434 mph)
2 Nov. 1965	Craig Breedlove	Spirit of America Sonic 1	Turbojet	894 km/h (555 mph)
15 Nov. 1965	Craig Breedlove	Spirit of America Sonic 1	Turbojet	967 km/h (601 mph)
23 Oct. 1970	Gary Gabelich	Blue Flame	Rocket	1,612 km/h (1,002 mph)
4 Oct. 1983	Richard Noble	Thrust 2	Turbojet	1,019 km/h (633 mph)
25 Sept. 1997	Andy Green	Thrust SSC	Turbofan	1,149 km/h (714 mph)
15 Oct. 1997	Andy Green	Thrust SSC	Turbofan	1,228 km/h (763 mph) (First supersonic land speed record)

A NEW ERA – THE JET AGE

At first, Craig Breedlove's record-breaking drive was considered an unofficial record because Spirit of America was a three-wheel vehicle and was not wheel-driven. But when it was recognized as a world record by the Federation of International Motorcycling, a new era of fierce competition for the land speed record began. In the two years from 1963 to 1965, five individual records were set and the land speed record swapped hands three times between Craig Breedlove, Tom Green (Wingfoot Express, 1964) and Art Arfons (Green Monster, 1964).

The tailfin measures 3.2 m (10 ft 6 in) from the ground and helps to stabilize the car so that it can travel straight.

The bodyshell of Spirit of America was built from a chrome steel framework covered by aluminium skin panels.

With thrust-powered cars such as Spirit of America, the wheels are only used to connect the vehicle to the ground. All the power comes directly from the thrust of the jet engine.

BIGGEST MONSTER TRUCK

BIGFOOT 5

In the mid-1970s, Bob Chandler started work on modifying his four-wheel drive Ford F-250 pickup truck. Sturdy workhorses like the F-250 could handle off-road driving, but Bob found that he needed something a bit tougher to cope with extremely rough terrain.

Among the upgrades he pioneered were a raised chassis, bigger axles and the addition of huge wheels capable of being steered independently. Slowly, piece-by-piece, his 4x4 truck got bigger and stronger, until it became the world's first monster truck. At a car show in Denver in 1979 his monster truck made its first public appearance with a name to match its huge scale: Bigfoot. The original monster truck was just the first in a long line of monster trucks built by Bob Chandler to have the name Bigfoot. In 1986, he built a new version of Bigfoot with three-metre-high tyres. Bigfoot 5 as it was named took the world record for the biggest monster truck ever.

Monster trucks such as Bigfoot 5 have engines designed to run on alcohol like a racing car.

Built with a 1996 pickup truck body and wheels from a massive military land train designed for driving in Alaska, Bigfoot 5 stands 4.7 m (15 ft 5 in) tall.

FIRST CAR CRUSH

In the 1980s monster trucks got bigger and more powerful, starring at car shows and competing in new monster truck sporting events. Bigfoot 1 pioneered one of the crowd-pleasing stunts that monster trucks perform at car shows: the car crush. In 1981, Bob Chandler tested out Bigfoot's traction power by driving over two wrecked cars in a field. The monster truck's massive weight crushed the flimsy cars under its huge wheels. When he repeated the stunt at a car show the following year the car-crushing craze caught on.

BIGFOOT 5

WHEN	1986
LENGTH	4.7 m (15 ft 5 in)
WIDTH	4 m (13 ft 2 in) with standard Alaska Tundra tyres
WHEELBASE	3.4 m (11 ft 2 in)
KERB WEIGHT	12,700 kg (28,000 lb)
TOP SPEED	139 km/h (86 mph)
POWER	149 kW (200 hp)
ENGINE	7.5-litre (458-cu-in) Ford F-250 460 V8 engine
NUMBER BUILT	1

Each 3-metre aluminium wheel and tyre weighs more than 1,000 kg (2,204 lb), so with a set of duals fitted (double tyres) Bigfoot can weigh in at more than 17,000 kg (37,500 lb) kerb weight.

FIRST ROAD-LEGAL SELF-DRIVING CAR

GOOGLE SELF-DRIVING CAR

The idea of a car that can drive itself goes right back to the early days of motoring. At the New York World's Fair in 1939, visitors were given a glimpse of how automated cars might work in a huge model called Futurama.

Built by General Motors the model showed radio-controlled electric cars automatically driving along a network of highways in a city of the future. Automated cars offered a vision of faster, safer driving, without traffic jams or crashes. It may have seemed like science fiction back then, but self-driving cars are a reality today and are being developed by many car manufacturers. In May 2012, the state of Nevada, USA issued the first licence for a driverless car to run on its roads. The car was a modified Toyota Prius kitted out with driverless technology developed by Google. To date, Google's fleet of experimental self-driving cars (SDCs) has clocked up more than a million driverless kilometres (miles).

Powered by batteries, this small electric car is designed with city journeys in mind and has two seats and a small amount of luggage room for cases or shopping bags.

SELF-DRIVING TECHNOLOGY

Many modern cars use some elements of automation, from anti-lock brakes to self-parking systems. Autopilots take cars closer to being fully self-driving, with automatic steering and parking. However, the driver in these cars can still quickly take over control with a turn of the steering wheel or a touch of the brake pedal. Google's latest experimental car does away with manual controls altogether, except for a stop and a start button, making it a true self-driving car.

More of a bus than a car, the French-built Navya became the world's first commercially available self-driving vehicle in January 2014. The Navya is a 10-seater self-driving electric shuttle, used for ferrying passengers around college campuses and hospitals, rather than out on the open road.

As well as adapting existing cars, in May 2014, Google unveiled its own self-driving car, which took the self-driving concept even further as it doesn't have a steering wheel and has no brake or accelerator pedals. It's a car designed for riding rather than driving – a bit like having a robot chauffeur.

GOOGLE SELF-DRIVING CAR

WHEN	2014
LENGTH	*2.5 m (8 ft 2 in)
WIDTH	*1.5 m (4 ft 11 in)
WHEELBASE	*1.8 m (5 ft 11 in)
KERB WEIGHT	*700 kg (1,543 lb)
TOP SPEED	Limited to 40 km/h (25 mph) for safety
ENGINE	Electric motor
RANGE	160 km (99 miles)
	* = approximate value

Video cameras and image recognition software allow the car to recognize traffic signals and other cars.

The car's computer systems can work out its position and destination on digital maps by using GPS – the Global Positioning System.

Radar systems at the front and rear automatically detect obstacles so that the car can react to them, including pedestrians or cyclists in its path.

TALLEST PRODUCTION CAR

ROLLS ROYCE PHANTOM EWB

Luxury cars, such as the Rolls Royce Phantom, are as much about comfort, elegance and making a big impression as they are about driving performance. Designed to be chauffeur driven, while the passengers enjoy the ride in its spacious and comfortable interior, the Rolls Royce Phantom EWB delivers that little bit extra when it comes to legroom and headroom.

The EWB stands for extended wheelbase and this version of the Phantom adds an extra 250 mm (10 in) to the rear passenger compartment. That gives passengers more than 1.3 metres (7 feet 7 inches) of legroom, which together with the power reclining seats ensures maximum comfort on any journey. To add to its impressive presence, the Phantom EWB is also the tallest production car in the world, with a height of more than 1.6 metres (5 feet 3 inches).

The bodywork is built around a welded aluminium spaceframe, which is both lightweight and strong.

The large rear "coach" doors open almost 90 degrees backwards, so that passengers can make a dignified entry or exit too.

ROLLS ROYCE PHANTOM EWB

WHEN	2005 to present
LENGTH	6.1 m (20 ft)
WIDTH	1.9 m (6 ft 2 in)
HEIGHT	1.64 m (5 ft 5 in)
WHEELBASE	3.82 m (12 ft 6 in)
KERB WEIGHT	2,694 kg (5,939 lb)
TOP SPEED	240 km/h (149 mph)
ACCELERATION	0-100 km/h (0-62 mph) in 6.1 seconds
FUEL CONSUMPTION	6.7 km/litre (15.8 mpg)
POWER	338 kW (453 hp)
ENGINE	6.75-litre (412-cu-in) V12 direct injection engine

FILLING THE SPACE

The extra space in the passenger compartment of the extended wheelbase version of the Phantom allows for extra-luxurious fixtures and fittings, such as fold down picnic tables, built-in TV screens or a refrigerator. The rear doors even have special umbrella compartments that are revealed when the door opens.

The Phantom EWB is hand-built at Goodwood in England and can be adapted to suit a customer's requirements, including the colour of the bodywork (there's a choice of 44,000 paint colours) and the colour of the leather seats and interior fittings.

The Phantom EWB is also one of the heaviest cars in the world, so it's a good job that it has a powerful 6.75-litre (412-cu-in), 12-cylinder engine.

LIGHTEST PRODUCTION SPORTS CAR

ARIEL ATOM

When it comes to delivering impressive acceleration, the Ariel Atom demonstrates that it's not just down to engine power – it's the ratio of that power to the weight of a car that counts. Originally developed from a student engineering project by Niki Smart, the British-built Atom was designed from the outset to be ultra light in order to deliver racing car performance.

With no roof, doors or excess bodywork to add to the car's weight, the strong and lightweight tubular stainless steel chassis is largely exposed. This minimalist approach gives the Ariel Atom an excellent power to weight ratio and pays off with stunning acceleration. The 2003 model, the Atom 2, with a kerb weight of 456 kg (1,005 lb) and its 2-litre non-boosted engine delivering 223 kW (299 hp) of power, could go from 0 to 100 km/h (0 to 62 mph) in just 2.6 seconds. The Ariel Atom 2 came out on top at a number of car-to-car acceleration trials in 2005 and 2006, beating a number of much more expensive cars.

The engine is mounted at the rear like a formula racing car. A rear spoiler provides downforce.

ATOMIC UPGRADES

There have been seven versions of the Ariel Atom to date, but they are all lightweight, no-frills cars with high-acceleration. The Ariel Atom 3 established a market for drivers who wanted racing car performance with the added motorcycle-style thrill of feeling the air rush by. In February 2008, Ariel introduced the Ariel Atom 500, an upgrade on the Atom 3 that pushed the racecar element further with a more powerful 3-litre (183-cu-in) V8 engine, plus carbon fibre panels and aerofoils. Capable of 0 to 97 km/h (0 to 60 mph) in 2.3 seconds, the Atom 500 is road-legal, but equally at home on the track.

The powder-coated steel chassis is welded together with triangular cross-pieces to maximize strength and keep weight low. Additional bodywork is limited to minimal aluminium bulkheads and fibre-composite panels.

ARIEL ATOM 3.5R

WHEN	2014
LENGTH	3.4 m (11 ft 2 in)
WIDTH	1.8 m (5 ft 11 in)
HEIGHT	1.64 m (5 ft 5 in)
WHEELBASE	2.3 m (7 ft 7 in)
KERB WEIGHT	550 kg (1,213 lb)
TOP SPEED	249 km/h (155 mph)
ACCELERATION	0-100 km/h (0-62 mph) in 2.6 seconds
FUEL CONSUMPTION	*14 km/litre (33 mpg)
POWER	261 kW (350 hp)
ENGINE	2.0-litre (122-cu-in) four-cylinder supercharged Honda K20Z engine
	* = approximate value

The KTM X-Bow (crossbow) is another ultra-light sports car. With a kerb weight of 790 kg (1,740 lb) it can do 0 to 100km/h (0 to 62 mph) in 3.9 seconds.

The ultra-light 2005 Caterham 7 CSR 260 weighs in at 530 kg (1,170 lb), which helps its 2.3-litre (140-cu-in) engine deliver a 0 to 100 km/h (0 to 62 mph) time of approximately 2.6 seconds.

The supercharger for the 3.5R's engine is fed by an air intake behind the driver.

Although it looks like a racing car, the two-seater Ariel Atom is a road legal two-seater sports car.

With no roof, a mini-windshield rather than a windscreen and its open-frame chassis, the Ariel Atom is exposed to the elements so driver and passenger need to wear a helmet and weatherproof clothes in rainy conditions.

FIRST CAR FASTER THAN 1,000 KM/H

BLUE FLAME

Experiments with thrust-powered cars began in earnest in 1928, when the world's first rocket-propelled car was tested by the German car manufacturer Opel at its test track at Rüsselsheim. Powered by rear-mounted rockets, the Opel RAK-1 accelerated from 0 to 100 km/h (0 to 62 mph) in just 8 seconds.

Just over forty years later, one year after a huge Saturn V rocket had carried the moon landing astronauts into space, another pioneering rocket car made the headlines by taking the world land speed record. On 23 October 1970, Gary Gabelich drove the rocket-powered Blue Flame across the Bonneville Salt Flats to take the record with the first car to travel faster than 1,000 km/h (622 mph).

Blue Flame had a semi-monocoque bodyshell with a tubular aluminium frame in the nose and an aerodynamically shaped aluminium skin.

The specially designed wheels were 0.88 metres (2 ft 11 in) in diameter and had smooth tyres to deal with the heat generated by travelling so fast. The car was entirely thrust-powered, so the wheels generated no movement themselves.

ROCKET POWER

Rocket engines are known as reaction engines. They create thrust by driving hot exhaust gases out of a combustion chamber. Ejecting this mass of high-speed gases causes a reaction, which is that the vehicle moves in the opposite direction. The rocket engine of Blue Flame was developed from earlier experiments with a rocket-powered dragster called the X1. This used just hydrogen peroxide as a fuel. Blue Flame used a combination of hydrogen peroxide and liquid natural gas in its two-stage rocket combustion engine.

REACTION ◄───── ACTION

The vertical tail fin helped to stabilize the car and was almost 2.5 metres (8 ft 2 in) high off the ground.

The engines of rocket cars such as Blue Flame burn for less than 20 seconds, but create enough acceleration and thrust in that brief burst of power to achieve incredible speeds.

NATURAL GAS INDUSTRY'S THE BLUE FLAME

The 1,001 km/h (622 mph) speed record over the measured mile stood for more than 27 years, only being broken by Richard Noble in his jet-powered Thrust 2 car.

BLUE FLAME

WHEN	1970
LENGTH	11.4 m (37 ft 5 in)
WIDTH	2.3 m (7 ft 7 in)
WHEELBASE	7.8 m (25 ft 7 in)
KERB WEIGHT	3,000 kg (6,614 lb) (including 1,200 kg (2,646 lb) of fuel!)
ACCELERATION	0-100 km/h (0-62 mph) in 1 second
FUEL CONSUMPTION	1 tonne (1.1 tons) in 20 seconds
TOP SPEED	1,001 km/h (622 mph)
POWER	26,000 kW (35,000 hp)
ENGINE	Two-stage rocket engine powered by liquid natural gas and hydrogen peroxide
NUMBER BUILT	1

WORLD'S WIDEST PRODUCTION CAR

CHYSLER CROWN IMPERIAL

Cars reflect the history of their times – and in America during the early 1950s car ownership rocketed. During this relatively prosperous period in the US following World War 2, saloon cars were status symbols used to show off how successful you were.

They were large and stylish, designed to make a big statement and had big gas-guzzling engines to match their size. This was in the days before petrol prices soared and before environmental issues made the headlines, when big cars for the big highways still seemed to make sense. One of the biggest cars of the period was the Chrysler Imperial, its flagship high-end luxury car. This rival to the Cadillac and the Lincoln was one of the highest-priced cars of its time. Top of the Imperial range was the 1954 Chrysler Crown Imperial, a statement car that also has the distinction of being the widest production car ever.

WIDE-TRACK WHEELED WONDERS

	CAR	WHEN	WIDTH	NOTES
	Koenig Competition Evolution	1985-1992	2.0 m (6 ft 7 in)	A modified version of a Ferrari Testarossa with a widened track.
	Lamborghini Aventador	2011-present	2.0 m (6 ft 7 in)	Widest car currently in production.
	Mercedes-Benz 770	1930-1943	2.0 m (6 ft 7 in)	Known as the "Großer Mercedes", which means large Mercedes in German.
	Maserati MC12	2004-2005	2.1 m (6 ft 11 in)	Only 50 of these limited-edition production sports cars were built.
	Pagani Huayra	2012-2015	2.0 m (6 ft 7 in)	Just 100 of these super-expensive sports cars with gull-wing doors were built.

COOL CAR

Another luxury feature that came as standard was what was then a state-of-the-art air-conditioning system. The Airtemp system was controlled from the dashboard and recirculated the air it drew in from outside as well as cooling it. This was the biggest air-conditioning unit available in any car of the period, yet it was quiet to run and very efficient. It could cool the interior of the car from a scorching 48°C (118°F) to a more comfortable 30°C (86°F) in just two minutes.

CHRYSLER CROWN IMPERIAL

WHEN	1949 to 1954
LENGTH	6 m (19 ft 8 in)
WIDTH	2.11 m (6 ft 11 in)
HEIGHT	1.64 m (5 ft 5 in)
WHEELBASE	3.67 m (12 ft)
KERB WEIGHT	2,400 kg (5,290 lb)
TOP SPEED	150 km/h (93 mph)
ACCELERATION	0-100 km/h (0-62 mph) in 13.1 seconds
FUEL CONSUMPTION	5.6 km/litre (13.2 mpg)
POWER	134 kW (180 hp)
ENGINE	5.4-litre (330-cu-in) Chrysler FirePower V8 engine
NUMBER BUILT	Approximately 77 Limousines and 23 Sedans for the 1954 models

The fully featured Crown Imperial had power steering, automatic gear-changing transmission, power disc brakes and electric windows.

The four-door, eight-passenger Crown Imperial was available in two body styles: a sedan or limousine. The main difference between the two was a glass partition to separate the driver from the passenger compartment.

A subsequent model's advertisement, targetting customers such as the super-rich, heads of state or film stars.

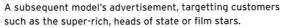

ULTIMATE ROCKET AND JET HYBRID CAR

BLOODHOUND SSC

The team that broke the sound barrier with Thrust SSC plans to return to the land speed record challenge with the Bloodhound SSC – a supersonic car that will travel faster than 1,600 km/h (1,000 mph).

That means the car will travel 150 metres (500 ft) in the blink of an eye and may literally be faster than a speeding bullet fired from a gun. The British-built car has been in development in Bristol, UK, for eight years. Following trials on a specially prepared 19-kilometre (12-mile) track in the dry lake bed of Hakskeen Pan in South Africa, the team will attempt a new 1,600-km/h (1,000-mile) speed record.

The four 91-cm (3-ft) diameter wheels are precision made from solid aluminium and will rotate 10,200 times every minute.

The final design for the Nammo hybrid rocket engine will most likely be a cluster of rocket combustion chambers.

BLOODHOUND SSC

WHEN	2016
LENGTH	13.4 m (44 ft)
WIDTH	2.5 m (8 ft 2 in)
WHEELBASE	8.9 m (29 ft 2 in)
KERB WEIGHT	7,786 kg (17,165 lb) fuelled
TOP SPEED	1,690 km/h (1,050 mph) theoretical top speed
ACCELERATION	Estimated 0-1000 km/h (0-621 mph) in 55 seconds
FUEL CONSUMPTION	800 litres (211 gallons) in 20 seconds
POWER	212 kN (23 tons) of thrust
ENGINE	Rolls-Royce Eurojet EJ200 turbofan jet engine, Nammo HTP hybrid rocket engine, Jaguar Land Rover V8 engine
NUMBER BUILT	1

The jet engine is mounted over the top of the rocket engine at the rear of the car. The air intake for the huge EJ200 turbofan jet engine is above the driver's cockpit canopy.

The driver lies down feet-forward in the driving cockpit towards the rear of the car. The plan is for Wing Commander Andy Green, who drove Thrust SSC, also to drive the Bloodhound SSC.

ENGINE ROOM

To achieve a speed of 1,600 km/h (1,000 mph) the Bloodhound SSC's engines need to generate an incredible 21 tonnes (23 tons) of thrust. The original plan was for Bloodhound to be solely rocket powered, but following tests a rocket and jet powered hybrid offered the best compromise between power and control. About half the thrust will come from a Eurojet EJ200 turbofan jet engine. This will take the car up to a speed of approximately 480 km/h (300 mph) before the rocket engine also kicks in. Fuelled by high-test peroxide (HTP) the Nammo rocket engine will add a 20 second burst of thrust to take the car up to 1,600 km/h (1,000 mph). A third engine, a supercharged V8 Landrover engine is also on board, powering the fuel supply to the rocket at over 40 litres (10 gallons) per second. Together the two thrust engines will supply more power than all the cars on a Formula One starting grid put together!

URT

GLOSSARY

Acceleration
A measure of how quickly a car can build up speed.

Aerodynamic
A car's shape is aerodynamic or streamlined if it has been designed to reduce air resistance (drag) as it travels at speed.

Axle
A strong metal rod with wheels that rotate attached at either end.

Cabriolet
A car with a roof that folds down to make the car open top.

Chassis
The chassis is the framework that holds all the parts of a car together. Older cars have a steel framework onto which everything from the engine to the bodywork is attached. Modern cars have an all-in-one framework called a monocoque body construction.

Concept Car
A car built to showcase a new design or new car technology.

Convertible
A car where the roof can be folded back or taken off to "convert" it to an open top car.

Coupé
A two-door car with a hard roof and enclosed interior that can seat two in the front and up to two in the back.

Cylinder
A cylindrical combustion chamber inside an engine where fuel is burned to push a piston that fits inside the cylinder.

Diesel
A heavier type of fuel than petrol that can be compressed and ignited without an ignition spark.

Disc brakes
A type of brake where a pair of brake pads are squeezed against the turning wheel so that the friction created slows the car down.

Drag
A force resisting a car's movement and slowing it down. Drag is caused by friction and turbulence created by the air a car moves through.

Four-wheel drive (4x4)
A car where all four wheels are powered either all the time or as a feature than can be switched on for specific driving conditions. Four-wheel drive provides better traction (grip) for off-road, snowy or slippery driving conditions.

Fuel
A substance that contains energy that can be released by burning. Fuels such as petrol and diesel are made from chemicals containing hydrogen and carbon and contain a lot of energy.

GPS
Short for Global Positioning System, this picks up signals from satellites orbiting the earth so that the position of a car can be accurately located.

Hatchback
A car with a door that opens upwards at the back to give access to storage space for easy loading.

Horsepower
A measurement of an engine's power, originally supposed to match the equivalent number of horses required. One horsepower is the same as 746 watts of power.

Internal combustion engine
A type of engine where fuel is burned in an enclosed space in order to release energy that is then mechanically transferred to turn the wheels of a car.

Kerb weight
The weight of a vehicle without the driver, passengers or baggage.

Monocoque
Modern cars use a strong and lightweight body shell called a monocoque as the framework on which a car is built.

Naturally aspirated engine
An engine where the air intake relies only on normal air pressure rather than being compressed by a supercharger or turbocharger.

Piston
A plunger that fits inside the cylinder of an engine and which is pushed up by the fuel as it combusts.

Production Car
A car made in quantity (more than 20) for general sale to customers, as opposed to one-off, limited edition or cars built to order for a customer. Modified or "tuned" cars are not production cars.

Roadster
A roadster is a speedy open-top two-seat sports car.

Saloon
A family car with two or four doors and a boot for luggage.

Sedan
A roomy car for four people with a boot for luggage.

Straight 8 engine
Also called an inline-eight engine. This has all 8 cylinders lined up in a straight line.

Supercharger
A compressor powered by an engine that squeezes and forces more air into the engine to boost its power.

Torque
Measure of the turning force created by an engine and applied to its axle(s).

Track
The distance between the outer centres of two wheels on the same axle.

Transmission
A gearing system that transfers power from the engine to the axles of the wheels.

Turbocharger
A device that uses a compressor driven by exhaust gases to squeeze more air into the engine and boost its power.

Turning circle
The smallest circle that a car can turn within with continuous forward movement. A measure of how manoeuvrable a car is.

V8 engine
An eight-cylinder engine where the cylinders are arranged in two rows of V-shaped pairs.

Wheelbase
The distance between the centres of the front and rear wheels.